★

"In a time of extreme polarization, Anthony Signorelli is building bridges. May Allah and Yahweh join together to bless his work and have mercy on us all."

Eric Utne, Founder, Utne Reader Magazine

★

"Freedom and independence are taken for granted by many citizens. Only when threatened does the importance of our rights become paramount. We need to understand and confront the abuses and excesses of capitalism. As citizens, we can no longer afford the ongoing attack on working families and the middle class at the hands of corporations and their government handmaidens. The future of the Republic and our democracy hang in the balance. Hopefully, this book will serve as a call to action."

Bernard L. Brommer, President Emeritus, Minnesota AFL–CIO

★

CALL TO LIBERTY

BRIDGING THE DIVIDE BETWEEN LIBERALS AND CONSERVATIVES

Call to Liberty

Bridging the Divide Between Liberals and Conservatives

by ANTHONY SIGNORELLI

SCARLETTA
PRESS

MINNEAPOLIS

Library of Congress Cataloging-in-Publication Data
Signorelli, Anthony.
    Call to liberty : bridging the divide between liberals and conservatives / by Anthony Signorelli. -- 1st ed.
    p.   cm.
    Includes bibliographical references.
    ISBN-13: 978-0-9765201-4-6 (pbk. : alk. paper)
    ISBN-10: 0-9765201-4-1 (pbk. : alk. paper)
    1. Liberalism--United States. 2. Conservatism--United States. 3. United States--Politics and government--2001- I. Title.
JC574.2.U6S54 2006
320.50973--dc22

                                                          2006031228

Book design by Chris Long for Mighty Media Inc., Minneapolis, MN

First edition | First printing

10 9 8 7 6 5 4 3 2 1

Manufactured in the United States of America
Distributed by Publishers Group West

For Ronald and Norma Signorelli,
who taught me the future can always be better.

For Lynn, Maria, and Victoria,
and the future world in which you will live.

Table of Contents

Acknowledgements

THIS BOOK IS BASED ON INFORMATION COMMONLY ACCESSI-
ble to the average citizen. My role is to put it together in a cohe-
sive form that others can understand. I write from the passion of a
well-informed and concerned citizen—deeply concerned about the
direction this country has taken since September 11, 2001—and I
realize our collective ignorance and fear have played a large part in
creating the current state of affairs. I am not an expert, or a political
scientist. I am not particularly active in any political party, although
I have friends in both major parties and some third parties. I vote
independent. This book is the outcome of a journey to overcome my
own ignorance and share my findings in the hope that other citizens
will similarly be moved to participate in the healing of the American body politic.

I have read extensively, and I am grateful to the authors whose
insights have helped me build an understanding of the materials
presented here. Books written by Friedrich A. Hayek, Ken Wilber,
Peter Steinfels, Olivier Roy, Paul Berman, and Michael Scheuer all
provided essential information or penetrating insight on which I
have relied. I thank each of them, and all the authors cited in the
book.

In addition to my reading, I have borrowed, developed and
worked over ideas with Jonathan Stensland, a dear friend and imag-
inative thinker who helped shape many of the core concepts and
ideas. I hope I have done justice to his contribution in the foot-
notes and citations, despite the difficulty of pulling apart hundreds

of hours of conversation, discussion, and commentary. Thank you Jonathan.

I am also grateful to Ian Graham Leask, managing editor at Scarletta Press, for an uncompromising commitment to excellence which at times exhausted and infuriated me, but nonetheless improved this book, its content, and its readability. Poet Thomas R. Smith served as an excellent sounding board and copyeditor, which I deeply appreciate.

I also want to thank many friends who have contributed in other ways, especially Robert Hill for his constant commitment, belief in these ideas, and leadership in financial support. He and Dawn Morningstar were two of the first to recognize what this project could mean, and they have been with me every step of the way since we first met. Kim Isenberg is a constant source of support, network contacts, and marketing ideas, and Marc Laurent and Nikki Carlson have creatively gotten this book the attention it needs and deserves.

Finally, and most importantly, I want to thank my family who patiently endured my absence, both physical and psychological, as I focused on writing this book. Lynn, Maria, and Victoria are the reason for writing it, and I dedicate the book to them. I have written it not as a creative expression of my inner being, but as an effort to help shape the kind of America in which they, and all of us, will live in the next few decades. Many voices together will make the change; I hope this is one small, but effective addition to that chorus of voices.

Introduction

"Polarization" is the new cliché in American political discourse: Red states/Blue states, Republicans/Democrats, liberals/conservatives. Many people lament the polarization, even though it seems to define contemporary political experience. Many Americans experience it in name–calling, shouting, and arguing at family gatherings. Tired of the ruckus, some families make deals: "Our family doesn't discuss politics. We prefer to keep the peace." Perhaps noble from the standpoint of the family, such decisions made in large numbers become damaging to the political culture of the nation. Such silence is interpreted as acceptance, even when it is not acceptance. One purpose of this book is to open the paths of dialogue and end the silence.

Americans have come to think of themselves as evenly and closely divided between liberals and conservatives. Partly as a result of two recent national elections, the dominant portrait of the American electorate looks like this:

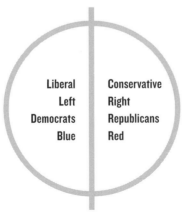

Liberal	Conservative
Left	Right
Democrats	Republicans
Blue	Red

We have accepted this divide because it is depicted every-where—TV news, magazines, talk radio, family debates, water cooler conversation. Polarized positions make for good confron-tational media coverage. But what if we are not as divided as some would have us believe? What if that image of ourselves is untrue, a false perception that impairs our ability to self-govern?

It is possible that the line dividing Americans can be drawn another way: horizontally. In this version, the people above the line remain dedicated to an American narrative that is widely shared and clearly understood, one that is defined by principles, one that is threatened today. Both sides—right and left—have their own extremists. Communists and eco-terrorists are examples of leftist extremists, while theocrats and fascists are right-wing extremists. Right-wing extremists have been in ascendance recently. Although one or another group of extremists may be dominant for a period, all Americans share a common story and a common heritage: those principles that make us uniquely American. This book has three main purposes: identify that heritage and those principles; clarify challenges to those principles and the forces of erosion in the body politic; and suggest tools for citizens to use in reclaiming American liberal democracy.

American Republic
Shared Principles
Liberal Democracy
Patriotic
Extremists

Communism
Anarchism

Fascism
Absolutism

The great American story is the unfolding, the development, and the fulfillment of Liberty's promise. Since the founding fathers created the original documents which organized our government and declared our principles, America has slowly but surely moved to fulfill the promise of those principles. No doubt we have had our failures, set-backs, and embarrassments, and committed our share of outrages—against African Americans, Native Americans, Mexicans, and South Americans, among others. But we have struggled to right those wrongs, and to expand liberty in religion, politics, and economics throughout our history. Until now.

Now we are a nation dominated by our own divisiveness. Families agree not to discuss politics because they prefer to maintain civility. Vitriolic rhetoric from writers like Ann Coulter is treated as newsworthy and given extensive coverage on media networks, while the reasonable voices in opposition are not heard. Shrill right-wing elites attack leaders of the Democratic Party,[1] while an ineffective left wing casts accusations of conspiracy against leaders of the Republican Party.[2]

Pulpits in our houses of worship are being debased by hate, self-righteousness, and calls to assassinate world leaders. Fundamentalist Christian ministers seek to create a "Christian" nation and eliminate what one commentator called the "five most dangerous words in the English language: separation of church and state." Many men and women of honest and earnest faith are confused by the cognitive dissonance between their faith, their God, their principles, and their ministers.

The deep division in the country is compounded by government policies that make little sense. A small group based in Afghanistan attacks America, so we invade Iraq. Meanwhile, five years after 9/11 our borders remain unsecured. In the name of "fiscal responsibility" we cut taxes for the extremely wealthy and borrow money to pay for the shortfall, thereby turning a budget surplus into an all-

---

1   See, for example, Brock, David. *The Conscience of a Conservative*. Crown Publishers, New York, 2002.

2   Recall Hillary Clinton's the "vast right-wing conspiracy."

time record deficit. Our dependence on oil makes us extremely vulnerable, so we give enormous, no-strings-attached subsidies to oil companies, who are making record profits.

These discontinuities and incongruities are confusing. Being of generous heart, many Americans implicitly trust our leaders. Others are more skeptical. The debate thus becomes polarized and personal, couched in the notion of a liberal-conservative split where "liberals" are demonized and true conservatives are increasingly disenfranchised. A growing part of the American population is falling silent. Many of us look at so-called liberals and so-called conservatives and mutter, "I'm not one of those."

But there is an antidote. There is a cure. The founding fathers laid out a vision and a set of principles, which year after year, decade after decade, era after era, call the American people toward the increased realization of liberty. Those principles and the Constitution stand as a beacon, drawing us from all corners of the country and challenging us to live up to them. Americans come to the Constitution and American principles from our businesses and jobs, homes and neighborhoods, churches and schools with all the knowledge of our communities and, despite our differences, we stand up for these enduring principles. This beacon, this common feeling and common commitment to freedom and liberty, is the bridge between liberals and conservatives. We are not liberals and conservatives first; we are Americans called to liberty. It is our vocation, our duty, and our responsibility to answer the call.

The American answer has always been liberalism, whether practiced by Dwight Eisenhower, Franklin Roosevelt, Teddy Roosevelt, Abraham Lincoln, Andrew Jackson, or Thomas Jefferson. It is a philosophy based on centuries-old principles that were in their time radical departures from the past, but which now constitute basic assumptions: private property, the Rule of Law, and the sovereignty of the individual are three basic principles. Liberalism is not the caricatured, hackneyed picture Americans have been led to in the last forty to fifty years. Rather, it is a philosophy of principles. American liberalism, and the liberal democracy we enjoy, are built on those enduring, objective principles. They are not values, nor are they individual assessments of importance that change with soci-etal winds, one's stage of life, or the opinions of a preacher. They are the principles that stand outside our individual assessment of their value, like the foundation pillars of American society. To oppose lib-eralism is to oppose those pillars.

This book is a crucible of thought meant to re-activate liberal American principles in the hearts and minds of the people. It mixes ideas across disciplines to create a tonic for the healing of the body politic. It starts by recalling the principles of liberal democracy, where they came from, and their comprehensive impact on society. Then, it addresses how those same principles are being challenged or eroded. There are internal political challenges, external enemies, and corporate economic structures which challenge and erode those principles, and which must be answered. Finally, I point a direction toward a notion of the citizen that we can all use, shape, and engage to help improve the political culture of the country.

The central theme is that thriving liberal democracy requires three essential modalities to be active and balanced: progressive, moderate, and conservative.[3] All three must be active, healthy, and legitimate. The progressive modality pushes for change and carefully defends social justice and equality of opportunity. The moderate favors compromise, gradual change, and tolerance. The conserva-tive understands that we possess wealth in natural resources which must be conserved, demands rigorous financial disciplines, and always asks what achievements from the past are worth preserving as we address the needs of the future. For these reasons liberalism is not the opponent of conservatism, but the beneficiary of conser-vatism. What is today being called "conservative" is in actuality a radical, right-wing agenda opposing the traditions, opportunities, principles, and liberties of the American story. The false but famil-iar notion of a liberal-conservative split in the nation serves only to cover the radical nature of that right-wing agenda.

---

3   Stensland, Jonathan. I first heard this notion of three modalities put succinctly by Stensland in private conversations, 2005.

The roots of this liberalism, which I have traced back to six-teenth-century Europe, include a new differentiation between the political, economic, and religious spheres of life and thought. Pre-modern thought fused these spheres philosophically and practically. Commit heresy against the church, and you could be tried for the religious crime of heresy as well as the political crime of treason.[4] Liberalism separates these philosophically and American liberalism separates them practically as well. The constitutional separation of church and state is an obvious example. Less obvious is the way in which the corporate structure separates the economic from church and state. The three great institutions in America are church, state, and business.[5] Separation and differentiation are essential to pre-serving liberty. When business, church, and state are all mixed up as one, totalitarianism is the likely result.

Conditions in America have arisen lately that are favorable for the rise of totalitarianism. Lies and deceits by leaders have confused the public dialogue in ways that make it nearly impossible to com-municate among citizens because we cannot even agree on what the facts are. Ruthless treatment of dissent in the Republican Party, in the Armed Forces, and in governmental leadership, together with willful mistreatment and incompetent management of detainees which leads to torture, have created fear and deep mistrust. The ongoing drumbeat claiming we are in a state of war when few people are experiencing the hardships of war create a cognitive dissonance in the people. Fiscal policies are making middle class Americans increasingly desperate for their economic well-being. The result is a deep confusion; a powder-keg of discontent across the country. All these are necessary conditions for fascism to overtake any soci-ety. It is nearly impossible to imagine that they are present in Amer-ica, but they are.

These conditions have recently intensified. Part II of this book provides insight into the rise of the radical right wing, the so-called

---

4   Wilber, Ken. *Marriage of Sense and Soul*. Broadway Book, New York, 1998.

5   Stensland, Jonathan. Stensland first named these three institutions as "crown, church, and charter" in private conversations, 2005.

war on terror, and the rise and conflation of corporate economic power with increasing corporate political power. The radical right-wing movement is now in power in Congress, the White House, and the judiciary, as well as in the institutions of business and American houses of worship. Our collective fear and ignorance of contemporary Arab culture and peoples has allowed our fears to be used against us, just as ignorance and economic insecurity are used to win our acquiescence to corporate priorities that do not align with our own individual interests, nor those of the nation.

For example, al Qaeda has declared war on America, including every American citizen, and has demonstrated an ability to attack us with devastating results. Al Qaeda comes out of an Islamic fundamentalism which deplores the notion of separation of church and state. It, too, developed decades ago. We may misunderstand al Qaeda when we believe its core issue is the Israeli-Palestinian problem, just as we may have misunderstood it when we believed al Qaeda and Saddam Hussein were on the same side. Al Qaeda is not made up of disaffected, impoverished people, but is an educated, Westernized, radicalized group at the forefront of Islam's clash with modernity. Their agenda, according to them, is to control nations and resources, impose totalitarian rule such as the Taliban in Afghanistan, restore the Caliphate as the leader of Islam, and drive the "infidels" from "Muslim" lands—what might be called "religious cleansing." If we can understand the intricacies of al Qaeda and its goals, we can prevent colossal American errors such as invading the wrong country, allowing insurgencies to flourish, or failing to act because the problem is too intransigent.

Right-wing extremism, terrorism, corporate domination. Contemplating these threats to liberty can lead to despair. But we need not despair. We need to be careful, we need to learn, we need to understand, and we need to act. Fascism can be fended off with the reassertion of liberal principle. A good first step is my proposal for a Free and Fair Elections Amendment to the Constitution that ensures auditable, verifiable, accurate voting and vote counting in every state, local, and national election. The liberal principles of the Rule of Law, checks and balances, and legislative oversight must be asserted against the arbitrary exercise and expansion of presidential power. In foreign policy, we can defeat al Qaeda only if we eliminate weak concepts like "war on terror" and replace them with solid, growing, and ongoing understanding. The ridiculous notion of a "war on terror" has resulted in unclear goals and poor efforts to define and defeat our enemy.

. . .

These important policy issues need to be addressed, but there is nothing partisan in this. In his book *God's Politics*, Jim Wallis recounts the adage that if your politician is making decisions by holding his finger in the air to determine the political winds, it does not matter if he is a Democrat, Republican, Green, or Independent. Nor does it matter if you replace him with someone from another party who also holds his finger to the wind. If you want change, you don't need to change your representative; you need to change the wind.[6]

Hence, the most important response to these challenges lies not in changing policy and structure, but in who we are as a nation and a people. It lies in our embrace of and engagement in liberalism—the philosophy of liberty—and in the engagement of our obligations and opportunities as citizens. Liberal principles are enlivened through exercise, engagement, and education. In the act of worshipping freely, we exercise religious freedom; in entrepreneurial endeavors or the organization of labor, we exercise economic freedom; in speaking, writing, reading, and thinking, we exercise political freedom. One need not carry signs and march in the streets, but it is our duty as American citizens to exercise liberty. Remember the old saying: Use it, or lose it.

The last section of the book points toward a new vision. As individuals we need to act. We need to overcome passive acceptance of a dangerous situation as if it were a mere "swing of the pendulum" and challenge ourselves to understand our situation; we need to

---

6   Wallis, Jim. *God's Politics*. Harper Collins, New York, 2006.

overcome our fears in order to find reasonable positions; and we must educate ourselves. We need to use sharper tools of thought and analysis to clarify the dynamics of political discourse, both public and private. Most Americans do not know what the Bill of Rights says, and so memorizing the Bill of Rights can become a profound act of patriotism. Organizing to make decisions in the public commons creates enlivened citizenship. Learning the skills of talking with those with whom you vigorously disagree is essential. Recognizing that the maintenance of liberty is at least one common purpose we share can provide the ground on which we come together.

American liberalism is the philosophy of the American spirit. We must revive American liberalism to prevent America from falling into the alternatives to liberalism such as despotism, fascism, totalitarianism, and communism. In order to accomplish that revival we must recall what liberalism is, identify and repel its opponents, and renew our collective commitment to its principles. We see ourselves as a beacon of hope and freedom. We see ourselves as a great liberal democracy. We see ourselves as a great nation of liberty. It is time for us to live up to that dream, and do the work required of a free people.

Recall the Story

CHAPTER I

The Demonized and the Disenfranchised: The Right Wing Steals a Word

THE REVIVAL OF AMERICAN LIBERALISM BEGINS WITH THE REC-lamation of the words "conservative" and "liberal." While the right wing has consistently demonized liberal principles for forty years, real conservatism evaporated from the public landscape of American politics. Through the "liberal–conservative split," right–wing activists demonize liberalism and steal conservatism in order to bestow a mantle of legitimacy on themselves: the label "conservative." The right–wing powers in America today are radical, not conservative, and profoundly illegitimate in a liberal democracy. Yet the right wing wins a perceived legitimacy because, by wearing the label "conservative," they are seen as legitimate by the general public. The right wing is not legitimate.

Liberalism and conservatism are being mischaracterized. Liberalism is portrayed as a caricature of an extreme ideology like anarchy and radical environmentalism, while conservatism is portrayed as a pro–fundamentalist Christian, imperialist philosophy. Both portrayals are grossly misleading, even though prominent individuals on both sides often act in ways that strengthen these myths. Liberalism should correctly be seen as the principled philosophy of America since its founding, and true conservatism seeks to protect and enhance those principles.

The right-wing movement consists of three segments: neocon-servatives, Christian fundamentalists, and the corrupt segment of the corporate elite. The right wing is strengthened by the fiction of a liberal-conservative split because the split gives right-wingers the "conservative" label which enables them to be perceived as respon-sible American citizens with responsible arguments, ideas, and agendas. But they are not responsible citizens. How can respon-sible citizens argue with a straight face that civil war in Iraq is in the American national interest, as some FOX News commentators argued in 2006? How can a Christian fundamentalist minister argue for the assassination of a democratically elected leader, as Pat Robertson did, and be taken seriously as a patriotic American? How is bankrupting the nation in the national interest? How can Hal-liburton executives seriously claim their no-bid contracts with the government are good for America when such contracts contradict all standards of good business practice? The perpetuation of the "lib-eral-conservative split" myth gives the right wing the title "conser-vative," which is perceived as responsible to ordinary Americans.

The reality is far different because progressives, moderates, and conservatives all serve American principles and worldview. And those principles are liberal. Right-wing ideologies fall outside the realm of what Americans commonly identify as American princi-ples. America as a Christian theocracy is not an American principle. Spying on Americans without warrant betrays a disdain of Ameri-can principle. Making war for purposes other than self-defense is not an American principle. Making a law to affect one person is not an American principle. Preference for church-based organizations violates the most basic American principle of church-state separa-tion. These all reflect right-wing actions and priorities. Progres-sives and most moderates obviously oppose such egregious actions, but so do true conservatives, many of whom cannot and will not stand for this. Most right-wing "accomplishments" stand in clear violation of the principles most Americans hold dear. Right-wing hatred of liberalism betrays the very meaning and soul of America, and stands far outside our real, historical culture.

Progressives, moderates, and conservatives all proceed from a *liberal* worldview.[7] Each standpoint sees certain issues clearly, while other problems go unheeded. Each standpoint possesses certain tools it uses regularly, while others remain unused. And yet, all three hold to the principles of American liberalism. We are not dealing with a liberal-conservative split, but rather a split between principled American liberalism, which includes progressive, moderate, and conservative, and some right-wing standard which lies outside the tradition of American liberal democracy. Such right-wing standards are not conservative, but something much farther to the right, approaching theocracy and fascism.

TRUE CONSERVATIVES DISENFRANCHISED

The evidence that the right wing is not conservative comes from the conservatives themselves. Many are deeply concerned, and occasionally they publish their thoughts. In Ron Suskind's book, *The Price of Loyalty*, Former Treasury Secretary Paul O'Neill portrays a real understanding of finances from a conservative perspective:

> ... the budget is often the only place where there is a true competition of disparate ideas—a competition over who will get the money and who won't. And the only way for that competition to work is for the budget to be finite. A ballooning deficit ... is a sign of casual thinking and tough choices not being made. Balancing a budget, thereby, is not just a matter of fiscal good sense. It compels companion virtues—such as intellectual rigor and honest assessment of the intentions that underlie action. Do you know what you're doing—and do you know why?[8]

O'Neill's view here is decidedly conservative in its high regard for limits, demand for rigorous thought, embrace of competition

---

7   Stensland, Jonathan. Private conversations.

8   Suskind, Ron. *The Price of Loyalty*. Simon & Schuster, New York, 2004, p. 280.

as a principle, and requirement of a certain kind of discipline. Yet O'Neill's statement is also profoundly liberal for all the same reasons.

The Price of Loyalty also tells the now infamous story of a 2001 oval office discussion over deficits, the impact of high deficits and accelerating debt, and the possible fiscal crisis portended by the economic policies of the current Bush administration. O'Neill argued vehemently for restraint and fiscal discipline. Cheney responded: "Reagan proved deficits don't matter." Initially shocked that his old friend Cheney would say such a thing, O'Neill considered the matter this way:

> I thought that, clearly, there's no coherent philosophy that could support such a claim.... I think an ideology comes out of feelings and tends to be non-thinking. A philosophy, on the other hand, can have a structured thought base. One would hope that a philosophy, which is always a work in progress, is influenced by facts. So there is a constant interplay between *what do I think* and *why do I think it* ....
>
> Now, if you gather more facts and have more experience, especially with things that have gone wrong—those are especially good learning tools—then you reshape your philosophy, because the facts tell you you've got to ....
>
> Ideology is a lot easier, because you don't have to know anything or search for anything. You already know the answer to everything. It's not penetrable by facts. It's absolutism.[9]

O'Neill reflects his adherence to liberal principles such as reason, the importance of facts, experience as a teacher, and fiscal responsibility. These stand in contrast to radical right-wing ideology which may try to claim them as its own, even though its principles are based on the literal truth of the Bible, free use of power and

---

9   *Ibid.*, p. 292.

authority, and American exceptionalism (the neoconservative idea that America need not obey the rule of international law). O'Neill, an avowed conservative, provides a shining example of how true conservative philosophy is completely consistent with true liberal principle, and how true conservative thought is completely inconsistent with the right-wing ideology, which today controls American government.

A second example of a disenfranchised conservative is Christine Todd Whitman, the former rising star of the Republican Party who fell out of grace as she fell out with the Bush administration, left office, and later published her book, *It's My Party, Too*. Whitman's perspective is that the "social fundamentalists" have taken over the party. She is clear about who they are: extreme Christian fundamentalists. "These groups [are] headed by people I call social fundamentalists, whose sole mission is to advance their narrow ideological agenda."[10] But such agendas, she says, are not the core values of conservatism and the Republican Party—values like smaller government, fiscal responsibility, and strong security. Whitman is very specific about how those values should guide policy positions:

> If we believe the government has a responsibility to be prudent in its use of taxpayer dollars and not run up huge deficits that will ultimately tax our children and grandchildren, we must push for fiscal responsibility and should seek to couple tax cuts with restraint on spending.
>
> If we believe that every woman has the right to make choices about her pregnancy, without interference from the government, we must not support appointment of judges who vow to overturn Roe v. Wade.
>
> If we believe that the Constitution protects individual freedom from an intrusive central government, then we must oppose a constitutional amendment to regulate or

---

10   Whitman, Christine Todd. *It's My Party, Too*. Penguin Press, New York, 2005, p. 3.

define marriage, and leave that matter where it belongs—with the states.

If we believe that protecting the environment is essential and is a public responsibility and a Republican issue, we must insist on advancing a pro-active agenda that actually results in cleaner air, purer water, and better protected land.

If we believe the United States has a vital role to play as the world's only superpower in leading the world both with strength and wisdom, then we must push for a foreign policy premised on the understanding that the rest of the world matters to us. We must advocate against becoming ensnared in nation-building enterprises and push for policies that engage us with the world community and show, in the words of the Declaration of Independence, "a decent respect to the opinions of mankind."[11]

The supposition in each of these statements constitutes the core creed of conservatism, but the current so-called conservative administration is going in the opposite direction on each of them. As head of the Environmental Protection Agency, Whitman's opposition on these and other issues led to her parting of the ways with the Bush administration.

Most of Whitman's "conservative" positions also belong to liberalism and liberal democracy. She writes of people who once "proudly called themselves liberal Republicans" to illustrate the former reach of the party. And then she asks:

So how, in recent years, has the party allowed itself to become captive of a collection of far-right forces, whose pursuit of their own narrow agendas makes it difficult to

---

11   *Ibid.*, p. 12.

govern and even harder to appeal to the great moderate center of the American electorate?[12]

In other words, both her Republican Party and the conservative values she holds dear have been lost, hijacked by the extreme right wing of the party. Millions of Republicans like herself elected and re-elected George W. Bush, but she laments their simultaneous disenfranchisement from the party. Whitman fears that the extreme right will take over the entire party if something doesn't change. "Preventing that troubling fate will take the emergence of 'radical moderates,'" she claims. Whitman's focus is on her Republican Party; the same risks and the same remedies may apply to America as a whole.

For a third example of disenfranchised conservatives, take Dave Durenberger. The former Minnesota Senator served during the Reagan era and is a true conservative—what I will call a liberal conservative, in that his liberal *principles* outweigh any right-wing *ideology*. He makes his views clear in a March 2005 interview with the Twin Cities weekly *City Pages*:

> Today, though—I'll cite Grover Norquist, who said something to the effect of, 'Bipartisanship is like date rape.' And that's what drives people now in the [Republican] party. They talk about freedom and values, but they really don't believe in representative government. They don't see that the country ought not to be divided in half. You're just looking at gridlock.[13]

Durenberger again:

> We use the words 'national security' to justify absolutely

---

12   *Ibid.*, p. 31.

13   Anderson, G. R., Jr., *City Pages*, March 9, 2005. Cover Story interview with Dave Durenberger.

everything that goes on in this country. And that's not American.

Imagine. A conservative Republican saying that using the words "national security" to justify everything is "not American." But Durenberger is a real conservative, not one of those using the word "conservative" to obscure some hidden agenda. He's not trying to hide a theocratic impulse, a tendency toward fascism, or a right-wing leaning. Durenberger's genuine conservative philosophy is at the heart of his perspective. Like so many conservatives, he is unhappy with how the conservative perspective has been stolen.

Here's part of Durenberger's response about religion in politics:

> Do they all come from their own churches and such? Yes. But look. I have very strong feelings about faith as a motivator. You can have your faith, and you can't just check it at the door when you go to work, but there's got to be enough respect to keep it out of what you do. When you start to rely on The Book to set policy, I begin to have a problem with that. I can't handle that one, the business of legislating your faith.... It can't last. It's not foundational as far as America is concerned; it's not foundational as far as representative democracy is concerned. You can bring your faith to your life and your work, but that should also include respect for other people and respect for other opinions.[14]

Many readers will have heard similar ideas from their "liberal" friends. But from a conservative Republican? Durenberger reminds us that America is a liberal nation based on liberal principles, and that liberalism is the philosophical basis of our democracy.

These three examples of genuine conservative philosophy illustrate the difference between real conservatism with its allegiance to

---

14   *Ibid.*

the traditions of American principle, and the false right-wing "conservatism" that presently dominates Republican Party politics and the American government. O'Neill, Whitman, and Durenberger all believe in the worldview of American liberal democracy, as do most real conservatives. Most Americans identify such values with the word "conservative," which is precisely why the right wing co-opted the name "conservative" for themselves.

LIBERALS DEMONIZED

If what we call "conservative" is not really conservative, then perhaps what we think of as "liberal" is not really liberal. Liberalism is not what you may think it is. It is not communism, it is not socialism, and it is not the great Satan that will undo a mighty nation. Liberalism is not anti-war demonstrators, flower children, 1960s drug mania, or even rock-n-roll. It is not political correctness, thought-police, or a passive position of righteous judgment. Liberalism is not haughty intellectualism, anti-globalization protests, tree-hugging, dropping out, or treason. It is not Hollywood sensuality. It is not labor unions, special interests, or even organic food.

Right-wing propagandists deliberately encourage these popular misperceptions of liberalism in an ongoing effort to unseat liberalism as the dominant worldview of America. The right-wing movement sets up such straw men as: liberal equals drugs, liberal equals debauchery, liberal equals prejudice against white men. The right-wing media repeats these equivalences over and over again to establish the connection in people's minds, and then hammers away at it for decades. Once the straw men are established, the right-wing commentators, preachers, and politicos swipe at them with a neoconservative sword, flatten them under a two-ton Bible, and declare victory. Middle Americans watch and think, "Oh! Look at that! I don't want to be one of those. I'm not a liberal!"

People who accept the label "liberal" do not always effectively dispel these myths. Indeed, they often seem just as committed to the perpetuation of the split as their apparent opponents. Many prominent voices align themselves more with the left than they do with liberty and liberal principles. When Cornell West, author of *Race Matters* and *Democracy Matters* and a strong voice for liberty, justice, and democracy stands with Hugo Chavez, the popularly-elected but apparently leftist leader of Venezuela, is it a stand for liberty or a stand for leftist politics? Many Americans question West's purpose and motive. When Michael Moore's movie implies a conspiracy surrounding the 9/11 attacks, many Americans ask, "Is this reason and analysis or left-wing propaganda?" Agree or disagree with West and Moore, but these positions and actions, in a society accepting of the demonization of liberals, reinforce perceptions of liberalism that feed the so-called liberal-conservative split.

Helped by the actions of such left-leaning leaders who are perceived as "liberals," the demonization of liberalism arises squarely from vile right-wing attacks on liberals and liberalism. Vitriolic right-wing rhetoric spreads hatred, fear, and misunderstanding, and is shockingly perpetrated with little or no effective public response.

Astonishingly, certain personalities of the far right get away with excoriating liberals as if liberals were not even human; in fact, this often lifts these writers and personalities to the very top of the right-wing power structure.

- Ann Coulter has claimed that to be liberal is to commit treason against America.

- Jim Gibbon, a U.S. congressman, said that liberals should have been shipped to Iraq to be used as human shields for our military.

Outrageous statements like these violate every sense of decency held by most Americans. They are cousins to related outrages, like the murder of doctors who perform legal abortions, or hate crimes. Whether for fear of disagreeing or some other reason, few say anything. Dare to protest in anything but a homogeneous group of like-minded people, and you will be disparaged. So, there is a deepening silence. Silence from liberals, silence from moderates, silence from moderate Christians, silence from Republicans, silence from progressives and conservatives, silence from Democrats. Our collective silence says more about the breakdown of the body politic than any statement could.

The result of this demonization is that few Americans identify with liberalism anymore. A 2002 Harris Poll indicated that only 19 percent of Americans identify themselves as liberals, even though we live in a great liberal democracy. Both our national dialogue and the character of our body politic are deeply disturbed when the people can or will no longer identify themselves as what they really are. The breakdown in the language underlying this disturbance compromises our ability to make clear distinctions, communicate, or negotiate. Reason, a pillar of liberal philosophy, suffers when the language is unclear.

THE THREE MODALITIES OF A VIBRANT LIBERALISM

Rather than viewing the wings of American politics as hostile to one another, I propose a re-imagining of the body politic. Americans share a heritage that comes out of centuries of liberal philosophy, and we subscribe to principles that are essentially liberal. Liberty is our calling, and liberalism is the story that unites us as Americans.

American liberalism is the one thing all Americans share, even though we are suspicious of the term. Most people accept its basic principles, which are delineated in the next chapter. And most people know the familiar story of the way in which Revolutionary America expressed the most profound ideals of freedom and liberty. From the Revolution to the abolition of slavery, women's suffrage, labor rights, and civil rights, most Americans warmly embrace the inevitable march of liberty through our history. This is the reason we call America a "liberal democracy," and we can and should be proud of the term. As one gentleman at a talk I once gave said, "So, what you're saying is, 'We're all liberals!'" Yes, we are all liberals, even if we are not living up to the liberal promise very well.

Liberalism is a philosophy with a five-hundred-year history. As our worldview, liberalism forms the foundation of American government, economics, and religion.[15] Our worldview is represented by our sense of fairness, justice, truth, reason, and inspiration. Liberalism is so large that it encompasses almost the entire political spectrum; progressives, moderates, and conservatives all belong within the grand tradition of liberalism.[16] Only the most extreme right-wing and left-wing movements find no home in the liberal worldview.

LIBERALISM

Progressive	Moderate	Conservative
Change	Compromise	Honor tradition
Fairness	Majority	What's good from past
Help less fortunate	Common sense	Conserve wealth
Distribute opportunity	Gradualism	Fiscal discipline
	Tolerance	

Re-imagining American liberalism requires that we look dispassionately at each modality of liberalism—progressive, moderate, and conservative—and recognize where the energy of the modality legitimately raises concerns and issues within the frame of liberalism. A re-imagined body politic demands that we recognize where the modality goes overboard and becomes illegitimate in the sense that it stops serving the aspirations of citizens. All the energies

---

15   Stensland, Jonathan. In private conversations, Stensland laid out the notion of economics, politics and religion as being three legs of a true ideology. I found the notion very useful, as it opened avenues of inquiry in understanding our current situation. The word "ideology" carries connotations that do not fit liberalism. Liberal worldview and liberal philosophy are more exact and definite terms which I use throughout.

16   Stensland, Jonathan. In private conversations, Stensland and I seeded the notion that liberalism includes progressive, moderate and conservative "modalities" (his term), and we explored them in some depth. Many months later, I wrote these descriptions and certainly include inspiration arising from those conversations. In writing, I introduced the notion of legitimate and illegitimate aspects of each modality as a way of clarifying the ideas.

deployed in our political debates have legitimate points to make; their illegitimate arguments serve only to whip up fear, confusion, and isolation. We must first understand the energy of each modality in and of itself, then hold its claimants and proponents accountable to the outcomes they claim it will produce. As citizens, this process requires our constant vigilance, education, and commitment to the renewal of our democracy.

THE PROGRESSIVE MODALITY

The progressive modality draws its core energy from the human capacity to hope. Hope implies improvement in the future and provides the momentum for forward movement, for progress and the expression of the human creative drive. Hope inspires us to act, and serves as the creative energy of entrepreneurship, art, and social and political activism. Hope, or the promise of progress, is the torchlight guiding the commitment of new immigrants to work hard for a better future; it spurs small business people to risk everything in search of a better eventuality for their lives; it inspires service to the poor, work to alleviate poverty, and even the work of missionaries. Progress flows as a political energy based on the notion: We can change this. We can do better.

Progressive energy is the source that builds things, and the driving force behind addressing perceived wrongs. Progressivism gave us the Hoover Dam, America's great bridges, the interstate highway system, and the space program. Some we may look back on as successful and good programs, and others we may later view as disasters. Either way, such projects come from a commitment to American progress and are paid for from the pubic treasury for the benefit of all.

Progressivism provides the lens that shows where the system is unfair, preferential, or exclusive. The Fourteenth Amendment, which guarantees equal protection under the law, was a progressive initiative. Abolition, woman's suffrage, the labor movement, and civil rights were all progressive movements. The progressive questions repeat themselves over and over again: What are we doing wrong? How can we do better? How can we be more fair? How can we release more of the spontaneous energy of liberty among more of our people? What is unjust and how do we fix it?

Legitimate progressivism encompasses the inspired energy of hope, the facts as we understand them, and the entrepreneurial creativity of the business community. It is legitimate because it is an integrated, connected energy that serves the needs of society to move forward and address its issues. Progressive sensibilities acknowledge that sometimes government needs to play an integral role in creating an environment in which liberty is optimized. Even as far back as the Revolution, people acknowledged the "public good," defined mostly as those activities that would serve the unalienable rights of man, a philosophical concept from the Enlightenment deeply embedded in the founding ideas of America. Quasi-governmental organizations were established to meet these needs, and resulted in early projects like the Erie Canal. The great projects are one part of the progressive legacy. Basic utilities like water, sewer, electricity, and rural electrification were also provided under progressive programs. Progressivism leads the culture in understanding the necessity of infrastructure for the freeing of the human spirit. Inspired by hope, it converts directly into real, on-the-ground projects that help people.

Real conservatives are wary of progressivism precisely for this reason. While trying to create an environment in which freedom, prosperity, and inspiration can flourish, progressive energy can go too far. When progressive sensibility spills over from guaranteed infrastructure—like building good roads—to an effort to guarantee *outcomes*—such as telling people where they may gather and with whom they may meet—progressivism leans away from liberal principle. In the hands of rigid thinkers and ideologues, *illegitimate* progressivism moves in the direction of totalitarianism as it asserts the control necessary to achieve those guaranteed outcomes. Such control leads progressivism toward dictatorial socialism or communism.[17] Any kind of totalitarian government or culture thwarts the aspirations of a people to be free, whether rooted in the right or the left of the political spectrum. Extreme progressivism makes illegitimate claims on behalf of "the people," and becomes itself illegitimate. Although it claims to be progressive, it loses its connection to liberalism.

For example, most people would recognize as absurd a proposal for equal income for everyone, but sometimes progressive ideas go in this direction. What about the idea that everyone should have a job? Or that all kids graduate from school with a B average? Progressive policies like welfare and the war on poverty became, in practice, a system of incentives and disincentives that created a cycle of poverty and entrapment for many people. Progressive visions can become unrealistic, and do more harm than good. At that point, the ideas may disconnect from reality, and also from the liberal principles at the heart of American democracy.

Progressivism sometimes labors under other less extreme misperceptions. As they move to the left, progressives tend to de-emphasize the importance of profit in the American liberal economic system. Profits are the fruits of creative economic enterprise, and their loss or denigration is contrary to the principles of liberal economics. Liberal economics requires that people are free to deploy capital and labor according to their own judgment, and to enjoy the fruits of those decisions. Progressives sometimes see profit as an obscenity that unfairly exploits the fruits of labor. Hence, progressivism will often view profit in opposition to economic or social justice. Such progressives are correct when the issue is exploitation. Exploitation of workers, especially when corporate structures are so endemic to our economic way of life, often

---

17   Hayek, Friedrich. *The Road to Serfdom.* University of Chicago Press, Chicago, 1944. Hayek's warning to the West centered on the idea that a sympathy for socialism can become nationalized fascism because of the control necessarily exerted to achieve the socialist goals. He saw socialism play a significant role in national movements in Germany, Italy, Spain, Greece, and Russia as each brought nationalistic dictators to power with the help of socialists.

figures into the profit equation, and such exploitation is anathema to liberty. After all, when unscrupulous corporations exploited labor in Europe, communism and Marxism resulted. But the confusion of exploitation with profit is a misunderstanding of the liberal economic profit principle. When they make this mistake, progressive positions become extreme and illegitimate. Liberalism demands a balance.

The old communist scare died with the Soviet Union in 1989, but many Americans remain nervous when they contend with progressive ideas that look collectivist. The fear is also raised when progressive ideas manifest as currents of American culture: for example, the sense of entitlement, victimization, political correctness, diversity, unionization, and universal health care. Legitimate ideas to ensure access to health care can get lost in illegitimate dreams of a nationalized system. The illegitimate currents are the Achilles Heel of progressivism: they are where progressives reach for the ability to control outcomes for others, thinking themselves better able to determine good behavior than people can for themselves. Such currents are illegitimate because they are the polar opposite to the principles of liberalism. Liberalism does not stand for victimization because it asks, what are you going to do about it?—thereby putting the responsibility for the solution on the individual, no matter the cause of the situation. The notion that a sense of political correctness will have thinkers and writers censor themselves in order to be accepted makes real liberal blood boil. In these areas, left-leaning politics joins with progressive impulses to create something very unattractive to the other modalities of liberalism. In the 1980s and 1990s, academic departments, non-profit organizations, and the media were frequently accused of succumbing to such pressures. In the 2000s, such accusations are more frequently made against far right-wing orthodoxy than they are against progressive positions.

Legitimate progressivism sees clearly the violations of American liberal principle perpetrated by the right wing, and champions change, fairness, and fact. Progressivism stands up for increased freedom and opportunity for everyone. The progressive style is to oppose its values to what it sees as "conservative" values. As a result, many progressives fixate on the wrongs of the right, which gives rise to an exposé-centered progressive press. Publications like *Mother Jones*, *The Nation*, and *The Progressive*, and radio programs like the *Al Franken Show*, *Democracy Now*, and *Ring of Fire* are examples. Just expose the lies, tell the truth, and progressives will win. But progressives are not winning because they are still locked in the liberal-conservative split, and the people who should be their friends in defending liberalism—the moderates and conservatives—are locked out. Progressivism sees what it sees, but doesn't see what is obvious to moderates and conservatives. Nonetheless, progressivism sometimes thinks it has the whole story and the only angle for opposing right-wing extremism.

The result is a progressive focus on short term issues and tactics. Progressivism shuns long term strategy and misunderstands the overall movement of the culture and body politic. It actually blinds itself to the bigger picture and is prone to want to elevate itself by insisting on being the replacement for the demonized term "liberal." A strategic, holistic perspective illustrates the mistake. The culture will benefit most as liberalism ascends, and progressivism takes its proper seat at the table—resisting the inclination to dominate over moderate and conservative styles of democracy—thereby declining the offer to be king.

THE MODERATE MODALITY

Moderate political energy lies at the heart of a well-functioning democracy, and, most of the time, at the heart of a livable society. The legitimate energies of moderation include compromise, gradualism, tolerance, consensus, and—somewhat paradoxically—self-interest. Moderate sensibility is about coming to accordance with one's neighbors. It seeks to develop solutions to problems that are acceptable to the majority. But in order to be moderate effectively, one must have a keen sense of one's own interest in relationship to the larger community—be that a family, neighborhood, state, or nation. Moderates understand that their own interest will be well-served by communal acts and decisions that serve everyone—a better community for all means a better community for each individual. And moderates are willing to work slowly and diligently to achieve the improved community.

Moderate energy serves liberalism because we tend to express our freedom best in a relatively stable environment. When America creates stability that serves the people, liberty can flourish. Business, intellectualism, art, politics, religion, inspiration, hope, love, and community all flourish best when change comes slowly. Moderate sensibilities recognize and embrace this reality.

Illegitimacy occurs when moderation becomes a creed unto itself. Real moderation sounds sleepy, but requires us to stay awake. Moderates must be alert to who they are engaged with, and whether or not the partner in compromise possesses real substance. Does the other party espouse ideas that are legitimate and tolerable? How does one compromise with a bully? An avowed racist? A Nazi? It can be like compromising with a drunk. The illegitimate moderate falls asleep and fails to take heed of his or her partners. He recalls his favorite words: compromise, tolerate, go slow. But his lack of vigilance leads him to compromise with tyranny, to tolerate the intolerable, and therefore to use moderation to betray the very values and principles at the core of this style of democracy. The moderate modality fails when the moderate person abdicates his responsibility to properly assess the opponent before entering negotiation; a classic example of this was Neville Chamberlain's passive accommodation of Hitler's demands prior to World War II.

The other illegitimate form of moderate sensibility occurs when self-interest becomes one's pre-eminent way of perceiving the world. We look at the world and say, "Well, I'm okay, so the world must be okay." This perspective betrays what Ken Wilber has identified as narcissism at the center of our culture—it all revolves around me.[18] My home, my job, my secure island that keeps the rest of the world away and my world neat and tidy.

---

18   Wilber, Ken. *Boomeritis*. Shambala, Boston, 2002.

Recent American voting patterns reflect this attitude. "My life is okay, I'm being protected from terrorists, my taxes are low. Guess I will vote the status quo." Such self-interested moderation played a large part in the re-election of George W. Bush in 2004.

At the same time, genuine self-interest is essential to the successful operation of moderate thinking. Compromise, gradualism, and tolerance all require a robust sense of self-interest in order to function. Genuine self-interest requires knowing oneself enough to recognize the power of an improved community in supporting and improving one's own life. In other words, self-interest promotes interest in finding solutions in the communities, families, and nations in which we live. Without self-interest, there is no basis for negotiation, no basis for the hard work of developing solutions and implementing them over time.

For the moderate approach, one compromises and develops a reasoned dialogue. Moderates have strength here, but they too often fall under the spell of the liberal-conservative split and believe that their right-wing opponents really share the moderate's desire to improve the world, govern well, and create fair and just outcomes for more people. True conservatives support these goals, but the right wing wants nothing of the sort. Genuine moderates do not bankrupt the government, tolerate incompetence, or send us to needless war.

Vigilance is required in order to ensure that moderate instincts do not collapse into a lack of consciousness or awareness of the challenges and opportunities that surround us. Millions of Americans have fallen under the spell of this form of illegitimate moderatism—most of them good, caring people. But in lowering their vigilance, many take for granted things that generations before us fought for, protected, studied, and earned.

The moderate spirit calls for balance, but its obligation is to be vigilant and realistic about the character of its political opponents. Insofar as the liberal spirit also requires balance, the moderate energy is an integral part of liberalism; it is a necessary, yet insufficient condition for the flourishing of liberal democracy.

THE CONSERVATIVE MODALITY

Conservative energy is an integral aspect of a healthy liberal body politic. Conservatism anchors the cultural base and keeps the progressives from flying too high and far. Real conservatives constantly ask the questions: What will we value from our past? As we move into the future, what do we not want to discard? How do we conserve the good that we have achieved? Are we really thinking well here? Do we know the limits? The founding fathers recognized the value of conservatism when they built our legal system on the foundation of English common law. They kept much of value from that slowly developed, widely held set of legal principles.

Conservatism conserves. It conserves the past, our traditions, our good ideas. It conserves wealth, profit, and free enterprise. The environmental movement is essentially conservative, even though it is considered a progressive issue today. Conservatism believes that government should be sufficient, but small. Real conservatism is suspicious of government intervention in our lives, tends to support and defend civil liberties, favors fiscal responsibility, and, more often than not, tends toward isolationism rather than interventionism and imperialism. Conservative thought insists on a real reckoning with limits, and insists on rigorous thought and an honest confrontation with pragmatic reality.

The tenets of real conservatism are clear. Suspicion over government intervention in our lives means caring not only about unreasonable search and seizure—Fourth Amendment rights—but also about intervention by legislating the private, reproductive lives of men and women; about sexuality, contraception, and abortion. Real conservatives abhor the invasion of privacy, no matter the content of the illegal search or legislative intrusion. Genuine conservatives—those liberals who view the world from the conservative modality—are consistent about liberal conservative principles and their application.

False conservatives use conservative rhetoric to hide their true intent. False conservative rhetoric appears as "turning the clock back." It appears when those goals are hidden as effects under a different, but related rhetoric. For example, "traditional values" may be a real conservative sentiment. But those words when used as cover or code, really mean, "Put the women back in their place; put the father back in charge; move the blacks out of the neighborhood, the schools, the jobs." Such views push the country backward. Legitimate conservatives do not seek to go backward.

Another form of illegitimate conservative energy often manifests as a pro-business mentality. The effect of most so-called pro-business policies, however, is the concentration of power, profit, and money in the hands of a few, usually through the structure of corporations. This illegitimacy has arisen periodically in American history. Think of the robber-barons and how they developed markets, monopolies, oligopolies, and cartels to effectively control the American economy and conserve their wealth by eliminating opportunity for others. The rhetoric may sound pro-business, but it is actually oriented toward retention of their own power, wealth, and position. This position leans toward a hybrid of aristocracy and fascism, rather than a real conservative discipline of fiscal responsibility.

Perhaps the worst of the conservative energy can be seen in the forces which have fought against our country's most important reform movements, starting with the Revolution. What were the Tories if not conservative? Too often, illegitimate conservatism has found itself on the wrong side of these critical issues: abolition of slavery, empowering working people, uniform voting rights for women and African Americans, the civil rights movement. In these cases, "conservatives" fought for the morally reprehensible on the basis that the practices in question have become a traditional part of the fabric of society. Historically, these illegitimate energies have existed in both political parties, just as the progressive and moderate energies have found homes at various times in each party.

Legitimate conservative concern recognizes the good in what we have created in America, and seeks to maintain it. We are blessed by the genius of our Constitution and the people who created it. We are also blessed by a strong heritage of Enlightenment principles, rational thought, religious inspiration, and entrepreneurial creativity—what used to be called "American ingenuity." We have a rich natural world in which to act, and many of our best traditions go back hundreds of years. Real conservatism seeks to conserve these traditions and resources and to maintain our wealth and our independence, both individually and as a nation. Conservatism is wary of change because of the danger inherent in losing what is good from our past. These impulses are critical for maintaining stability in the political, economic, and religious spheres in which we operate, and where our real, liberated spirit can be free.

LEGITIMATE AND ILLEGITIMATE

No doubt some will complain that the charge of illegitimacy is too harsh. It is not. The alternatives to liberal democracy are not legitimate to an America committed to emancipation, freedom and liberty. Communism, theocracy and fascism are not legitimate enterprises for America. Despotism and cronyism are not legitimate for America. Aristocracy is not legitimate for America because we are a "government of the people, by the people, and for the people." And yet, these ideological and political systems vie with liberal democracy. Any American theory or concept that argues there is a legitimate alternative to liberalism is false. True conservatism cannot be such an alternative because it is itself a creation of liberal democracy. Radical right-wing extremism ultimately becomes fascism or totalitarianism.

In order for these three styles of democracy to thrive again, Americans need to recognize as false the liberal-conservative split governing our political dialogue and characterizing the body politic. The false framework of the split provides a home for welcoming right-wing values and concerns. Whatever its origin, the liberal-conservative split has two clear effects:

- First, by demonizing liberalism, it disempowers liberalism as the dominant worldview in America. A disempowered liberalism results in an intellectual vacuum, which the right wing backfills with ideas that serve its interests: the unitary executive, the "values voter," the ownership society, and the constant drumbeat of fear.

- Second, the split enables the right wing to steal the legitimate name "conservative" and put it on an illegitimate, radical right-wing agenda, thereby making that agenda appear legitimate, palatable, reasonable, and mainstream.

The real values, concerns, and positions of the right-wing agenda are rarely stated clearly and honestly because they would not be supported by the American people. Yet they are reflected in governmental policy. They include: transferring wealth from the middle class to the corporate and super-rich; invading a country on trumped-up evidence for reasons as yet unstated; secret programs to spy on Americans without warrants in violation of the Constitution; gutting regulations—and enforcement—which protect workers, the environment, and the health of our people; bankrupting the government. How do these and so many other actions of the current government serve the people, be they progressive, moderate, or truly conservative? They don't. These extreme right-wing policies reflect the true ideologies of the right-wing movement. The word "conservative" has been hijacked to give the perception of legitimacy to absurd policies that reflect non-liberal, non-American, non-democratic principles. If nothing else, the actions of the present Bush administration demonstrate that America has much to lose.

Although many people in business, politics, and religion live by a commitment to liberal principles, the nature of those principles has become mostly unconscious in American culture. This unconsciousness means that while American liberalism activates many people across the different styles of democracy, the philosophy and ideas of liberalism remain underdeveloped in the psyche of contemporary culture. We need to deepen our understanding of liberalism and develop its ideas in order to revive its spirit in our culture and our politics.

THINGS TO REMEMBER

- There is no liberal–conservative split. The idea demonizes so-called liberals and disenfranchises true conservatives.

- Liberalism is what holds us together as Americans. It is our shared narrative.

- Progressive, moderate, and conservative are all modalities of liberalism.

- Each modality has its strengths and legitimate contributions, and also its illegitimate shortcomings.

- Legitimate progressivism champions hope and change, but the illegitimate guarantees outcomes and leads to a culture of entitlement, victimization, and political correctness.

- Legitimate moderate energy seeks compromise and builds from a sense of self interest, but the illegitimate slides into complacency or naiveté about the world and one's opponents.

- Legitimate conservatism upholds and protects cherished principles, understands limits, and conserves wealth and resources. Illegitimate conservatism becomes arrogant, slides into a backward longing for "the good old days," and often hides racial or gender based bias and fear.

At this point, a natural question arises: So, what is liberalism? We will begin to answer that in the next chapter, Principles of Liberalism.

CHAPTER 2

Principles of Liberalism

IF YOU THINK OF LIBERALISM AS A HOTBED OF RADICALISM, CON-sider these outlandish *liberal* principles: Private property, Rule of Law, individual sovereignty.[19] These were radical ideas four hundred years ago, but today we take them as the bedrock on which our culture, our economy, and our way of life rest. With basic liberal ideas like these, Enlightenment thinkers such as John Locke, Adam Smith, and Jean Jacques Rousseau had a profound influence on the colonists who were busily declaring independence, establishing a government, and building a new nation. The history of America, from its founding until now, is the history of the continuous attempt to live up to and fulfill the promises of liberal democracy and liberal principles.

Principles are not values.[20] Principles are objective and enduring; they exist outside one's personal judgment. Principles change slowly over centuries or millennia. In contrast, values are individualized and subjective, based on the individual's assessment at any given time, and reflect the individual's imperfect and changing knowledge and perspective. Our values change as we grow, as the

---

19 Stensland, Jonathan. Private conversation. We discussed the role of private property and the Rule of Law.

20 Stensland, Jonathan. Private conversation. The distinction between principles and values is an important clarifying idea I borrowed from these conversations.

country changes, and as new challenges arise. Change in values is natural and necessary, but it makes values a frivolous foundation for cultural development.

Principles stand outside the value equation in the underlying structure of society. You may or may not value private property, but it remains a principle to which we are all subject. You may or may not value Rule of Law, but it endures as a principle of America's liberal democracy.

We have to reach into history and bring the concept of liberal American principles into the present. The principles on which the nation was founded are what separate us, free us, and make us who we are as a people. If we do not know our own principles, we risk losing them in the worst possible way: through ignorant complacency. American liberal principles are too precious to let them fade away as a result of our current apathy.

Based on Enlightenment principles and their own recent experiences, American revolutionaries formulated the most famous statements of American liberal principle—the Declaration of Independence, which gave America the notion of unalienable rights of all people; the Constitution, which separated governmental powers to provide checks and balances between the three branches of government and the voters; and the Bill of Rights, which specifically enumerated many of the unalienable rights and made them clearly applicable to all citizens. This chapter provides a basic introduction to the principles of American liberalism which many of us know, but have forgotten.

PRIVATE PROPERTY

The principle of private property is one of the central pillars of liberal society, the mechanism by which enormous power is wrested from the aristocracy and nobility and placed in the hands of the people. Private property transfers wealth and power to the people, and provides the means for the creation of wealth which underlies the entire economic system. It establishes the capital base of the individual family, and fuels entrepreneurship, financial security, and other aspects of economic liberty.

Various concepts of property date very far back in European history, but private property—as an alternative to the feudal system of property—began to emerge with the Magna Carta in England in 1215, and spread through Europe during the Renaissance. As with so much liberal thought, the issue was debated by philosophers—Thomas Hobbes, James Harrington (later celebrated by John Adams), John Locke, William Blackstone, and David Hume were all involved. In the 1600s, Harrington clearly identified private property as an instrument which could be used to disempower tyranny. These liberal ideas have all been long-established—although treated differently at different times—in European thought and history.

At the outset, private property ownership was a radical idea which challenged an arbitrary land tenure system previously dependent on the whims of the king and the nobility. If an individual holding tenure of land under this system committed even a slight offense against the king, and the king then felt compelled a year or two later to reward someone else, and looked for land to grant, he might recall the offense. The land could then be taken away and bestowed on the "worthy" man.[21] The result was unpredictable, arbitrary control of the land.

The concepts of title and private ownership remove the arbitrary power of the aristocracy to determine land ownership, and profoundly empower the people; changes in land tenure occur by way of transactions between people rather than by royal or noble decree. The wealth represented by the land is freed as a source of investment capital, and landowners are enabled to act on their own behalf. Today, we accept this situation as a basic assumption, but it was not always that way, and still is not in many parts of the world. Looking at much of the Third World one can see the results of economies built without private property principles.

---

21   Stensland, Jonathan. Private conversation.

Hernando de Soto, president of the Institute for Liberty and Democracy in Peru, and author of *The Mystery of Capital*,[22] documents the lack of private property structures in Third World urban areas as a major factor contributing to the creation of a permanent underclass in the shantytowns of Mexico City, Lima, Rio de Janeiro, Bombay, and other areas around the world. Millions of people in these cities essentially live as squatters who own nothing. In every case, the lack of a functioning private property system contributes to the squalid poverty of these cities. The formal systems of the national governments are so unwieldy, complicated, bureaucratic, and inaccessible as to render them irrelevant to the majority of the people, who cannot claim ownership of the land on which they live, and cannot transfer control of it.

De Soto's analysis shows that the lack of workable private property systems in such places has effectively locked up trillions of dollars in wealth—wealth that cannot be accessed, leveraged, or used by anyone. This frozen capital gives rise to whole new societal structures, most of them informal. The shantytowns develop their own unofficial enforcement mechanisms, their own informal police, their own markets and tariff systems, and other economic structures to establish some sense of ownership, order, and stability. Gangs, neighborhood bosses, and other power centers emerge in the midst of the official power vacuum.

When this happened in America, we called it the "Wild West." One aspect of the American genius is that every time the population expanded into new areas, private property became the guiding principle establishing tenure on the land. The homestead programs, common law and squatter's rights were all part of the infrastructure of private property ownership. There was a very dark side to this: the land kept being taken from the Native Americans by the U.S. Government, primarily by war. Conquest, the dominant pre-modern tool for acquiring wealth, still functioned in the modern liberal democracy of America, and it was thoroughly exploited. Once land

---

22   De Soto, Hernando. *The Mystery of Capital*. Basic Books, New York, 2002.

was under the control of the U.S. government, it was systematically put into the hands of the people to be held as private property within the society. Hence, private property resulted in an enormous freeing of capital that has fueled the American economy.

De Soto's analysis helps us to see the critical importance of private property in the creation and maintenance of a liberal economic system. His groundbreaking research demonstrates that the lack of formal property systems in many Third World nations is an underlying cause in the creation and perpetuation of abject poverty and shantytowns. All Americans should consider this and ask themselves what is happening to the principle of private property in American society today? Do we need to be concerned?

Here, the threat posed by domination of the economy by corporate enterprise can be seen as a clear, albeit eventual, threat to liberal principle. Corporate land ownership moves land out of the hands of the people and places it in the hands of an executive class which then exercises arbitrary tenure over it. In a sense, corporate ownership establishes "fiefdoms," where land is taken out of the system and handed over to an "aristocratic" class. In most cases, the land never reverts to individual ownership, but is held in perpetuity by one corporation or another.

De Soto does not clearly address corporate ownership in the Third World. However, it is the primary tool for disenfranchising the people from their land and ensuring permanent subjugation of the population. The good land is taken from the indigenous people and descendants of immigrant farmers, often by force. The formal property system supports this theft by making it virtually impossible for the lower classes to assert any property rights. Denied ownership of the land, the people become only a labor pool while corporate or government interests exploit the land.

Starved of capital at the individual level, a liberal economy becomes nonfunctional. If the liberal economy cannot function, liberty cannot flourish because the people cannot enjoy economic liberty. Poverty flourishes where liberty wanes.

Tragically, the principle of private property is being hijacked from the American people. While tens of millions of people still own their homes, agricultural, forest, mining, and commercial land ownership is being incrementally concentrated in the hands of corporations, and wealth is concentrated in the stock market via 401k accounts, mutual funds, and IRAS, putting that wealth effectively under the control of corporations.

Beyond the obvious concentration of property and wealth, the problem is more direct and local. The stores, restaurants, and service stations that dominate suburban America are so ubiquitous as to make one suburb essentially indistinguishable from any other. Many decry this as a homogenization of culture; it is also a menace to our economic freedom.

In suburban development, an increasing proportion of the properties are controlled by REITS—real estate investment trusts—an entity created in the 1970s which enables corporations to acquire large empires of land ownership.

Many do not yet personally feel constrained by the concentration of property—land, wealth, intellectual property, and genetic codes—in corporate hands. But such concentration directly contradicts the principles of liberalism on which the nation is founded. The Revolution took property away from the King and put it in the hands of the people. Throughout more than two hundred years of American history, we have slowly transferred that property into the hands of large corporations, thereby giving away the keys to our freedom. The eventual effects of concentrated corporate ownership appear in the same shantytowns De Soto studied.

The principle of private property is basic to liberalism insofar as it assigns property rights to the people, not to kings or their representatives, and not to giant, faceless corporate entities. The freedom of the people is built on an edifice of principles that includes private property as a cornerstone. Take private property away, and the result is either De Soto's shantytowns or a decrepit and backward Soviet Union. In neither case are people economically free or inspired.

RULE OF LAW

The Rule of Law was succinctly articulated by Immanuel Kant, "Man is free if he needs to obey no person but solely the laws." The Rule of Law frees citizens from the arbitrary or discretionary rule of individuals—kings, tyrants, communist planners, and despots—by establishing rules which create a stable, predictable environment within which people can act. It makes the actions of other people and the state reasonably predictable so that economic, political, religious, and social actions can be undertaken without fear of capricious exercise of authority to thwart one's efforts. The Rule of Law is not merely the bestowal of "legality" on decisions or actions; it is a deeper principle whose objectivity and uniformity is its central feature enabling liberty to flourish.

Nobel Laureate Friedrich A. Hayek,[23] in his 1944 classic *The Road to Serfdom* wrote:

> Nothing distinguishes more clearly conditions in a free country from those in a country under arbitrary government than the observance in the former of the great principles known as the Rule of Law. Stripped of all technicalities, this means that government in all its actions is bound by rules fixed and announced beforehand—rules which make it possible to foresee with fair certainty how the authority will use its coercive powers in given circumstances and to plan one's individual affairs on the basis of this knowledge.[24]

When the action of the state is pre-determined by law, citizens are enabled to plan their individual conduct with a reasonable ability to predict state action in regard to that conduct. The framework is understood, and liberty flourishes. Freedom is the ability to decide for oneself one's own actions within an understood framework of laws, rewards, and consequences. Planned or despotic societ-

---

23   Hayek's work was introduced to me by Jonathan Stensland in early 2005.
24   Hayek, *op. cit.*, p. 80.

ies rarely undergo economic or political development because citizens are not free to develop their resources. The Soviet Union was an example of the planned society, Zimbabwe currently exemplifies the despotic.

Although it is a complex concept, The Rule of Law has four primary features. It is:

- **Nondiscretionary:** Rule of Law is objective, not subjective. It eliminates arbitrary or discretionary decisions.

- **Announced beforehand:** Rule of Law enables citizens to predict the manner in which the state will and will not act with regard to the citizen's affairs.

- **Uniformly applied:** Law applies to everyone; no person is above the law. Rule of Law has general applicability; it is not specific, nor exceptional.

- **Uniformly enforced:** Law is enforced evenly and equally on all citizens.

The primary function of the Rule of Law is to remove individual judgment or discretion in the wielding of the state's power. Ultimate authority is vested in the law itself, rather than in the judgment or discretion of a single person. Such law is objectively made, stated in public, easily knowable by the citizenry, and dependably enforced. As a result, individuals know what actions will get them into trouble with the state and what behavior is anticipated in order to stay out of trouble. The individual can act and make commitments with the confidence that economic, political, and religious competitors are not receiving unfair advantages. Drive on the wrong side of the road and you will be arrested; drive on the right side, and you will not encounter the power of the state. No one has the special privilege of driving down the center where there are no other cars at all.

In societies that are not under the Rule of Law, decisions of the state are discretionary and arbitrary. The state acts when an individual in authority *decides* to act, not when permitted or necessitated by the law. No man is free in such a state. No man can predict what is legal or illegal, allowable or unallowable, because those decisions are left up to the discretion of an individual. In pre-modern times, these powers were vested in a king or a feudal lord. In modern times, they are often vested in the authorities of state-run economies like the former Soviet Union, death squads or militaries run amok, or in the corruption of public institutions for private gain; especially through bribery, blackmail, and paying "fees" to get things done. These problems are commonly seen in those Third World countries where there is little tradition of Rule of Law.

Because the law is objective, it applies to everyone—even presidents, congressional representatives, and judges. The universal applicability of the law is central to its proper function, and where exceptions begin to be made, the Rule of Law is eroded.

A critical distinction must be made between Rule of Law and "legality." Just because an action is "legal" does not mean it is in conformity with the Rule of Law. To the extent that a constitutional body creates a law that confers discretionary rule or power to an individual or governmental position, it is not conforming to the Rule of Law. Laws that confer such power are the basis of the "legal" legitimacy of despots and dictators—the dictator convinces a legislative body to confer enormous discretionary power on him, or the dictator declares a crisis that enables him to take such power. In most cases, such moves are, strictly speaking, "legal" but in no way conform to the Rule of Law. The vesting of subjective, discretionary authority in an individual creates inherent arbitrariness in the law. As the arbitrary potential increases, the liberty of the citizens decreases because there is no way to reasonably predict the actions of the state. In other words, while a legislative act may be "legal" or "lawful" in conferring arbitrary or discretionary power on a government official, such an act is not consistent with Rule of Law.

The rhetoric of the current Bush administration defends a broad range of actions as "lawful." American citizens ought to be wary. While it is possible that the government's treatment of detained prisoners and its program of spying on Americans are "lawful," they are clearly not consistent with the liberal principle of Rule of Law. In both cases, laws and findings have created a legal framework to justify the legal case for what they are doing, but the effect is to put discretionary power for these programs in the hands of the president. He alone decides if they are being properly administered. He alone decides if someone is an "unlawful combatant" and therefore subject to detainment at Guantanamo without any recourse to justice or legal representation. The President has argued it is legal, and he has argued the merits of the need. Reasonable people can disagree about the legality and the merits, but there is no question that the president's continued accumulation of discretionary power is counter to one of the fundamental principles of liberty: the Rule of Law.

Arbitrary enforcement can also undermine the Rule of Law. Enforcement of the law is the responsibility of the executive branch. Lack of uniform enforcement necessarily increases the arbitrariness and preferential aspect of the law. For example, the IRS is enforcing exemption rules against major left-wing churches who preach peace from the pulpit. The IRS claims such preaching is an overt political act which contradicts the church's tax-exempt status, and targets large "liberal" churches. To claim a "balanced" approach, the IRS enforces the same rule against the smallest, most inconsequential churches of the right wing while many large right-wing churches blatantly tell people how to vote. This is selective, arbitrary enforcement of the law. When Vice President Cheney was alleged to have intervened to stop enforcement of environmental regulations against mining companies, it was discretionary law enforcement. When government in general is so under-funded that it cannot achieve uniform enforcement, the result is arbitrary enforcement, the behavior of the state is no longer predictable, and liberty is diminished. The dependability of enforcement is not based on objective criteria, but on one's relationship with certain individuals in the administration.

Liberal democracy and liberal society require the Rule of Law to function properly. As governmental action is increasingly based on individual discretion, government becomes arbitrary, despotic, and dictatorial. Conversely, liberty flourishes under the Rule of Law because it puts the decisions for people's behavior in the hands of the people themselves. The Rule of Law is a bedrock, an old time liberal principle; one which we must guard vigorously.

SOVEREIGNTY OF THE INDIVIDUAL

Another key liberal principle which underlies our governmental structure is the sovereignty of the individual. This concept arose with liberalism: that each and every human being enjoys sovereignty, responsibility, freedom to assert, autonomy—in other words, "... is endowed by his creator with certain unalienable rights ..." Individuals matter. This was a revolutionary idea.

Before liberal government came along, a nation's inhabitants were its "subjects." *Webster's Third International Dictionary* defines subject as, "one that is placed under the authority, dominion, control, or influence of someone or something." Ordinary people were subjected to the whims and concerns of an aristocracy, the king, their lord, their duke, their count. The entire infrastructure of the aristocracy was built on the hierarchy of subjects.

Modern Americans think of themselves as citizens. Everyone is a citizen. Rich and poor. Labor and owners. Urban and rural. We take this idea for granted, forgetting that it was not always the case, and usually unaware of the revolutionary aspect of the word. "Citizen" reflects the autonomy of the individual and a sense of mutual responsibility. In its simplest definition, the word refers to a member of a state. But the larger meaning, according to Webster, is, "a native or naturalized person of either sex who owes allegiance to a government and is entitled to reciprocal protection from it and to enjoyment of the rights of citizenship." The critical idea is *reciprocity* between the individual and his or her government. Citizens are not subjected to anyone, but rather enter into a relationship with government, a relationship defined by mutual obligations of allegiance and protection. In a liberal world individuals are full citizens; they are no longer mere subjects in a world of aristocrats.

Each person becomes a sovereign, individual actor in that world. Each one can think, live, pray, and sing as he wants to, and the right to exercise these freedoms is the key to the possibilities of

47

what it means to be human. The optimization of individual freedom is a necessary element in optimizing societal freedom. Any affront to the sovereignty of the individual is an affront to freedom and liberty.

The notion of the sovereign individual has played a role in many historical events, but it entered the American sphere most decisively through the writ of *habeas corpus*. The term means "you (may) have the body." Habeas corpus stretches back to ancient times and refers to the requirement that a lower authority present a person they hold under arrest to a higher court or authority. Habeas corpus was first used to protect individual liberty in Europe in the late Middle Ages and early Renaissance and, over time, it became the accepted procedure for checking illegal imprisonment of individuals by local authorities. The British Habeas Corpus Act of 1679 established the procedures through legislation, and the rights of the writ grew and extended further in America through the Bill of Rights and much later in the Miranda warning and other stipulations of defendant's rights. Even today, habeas corpus provisions are being debated extensively in relation to the detention of so-called "unlawful combatants" at Guantanamo Bay, Abu Ghraib, Bagram Air Base in Afghanistan, and secret CIA prisons in eastern Europe and elsewhere.

As liberal principles developed and the value of individual life increased in public awareness, habeas corpus became a tool individuals could use to defend their sovereignty—forcing arresting authorities to charge them with a crime before a judge or let them go free. To arrest a person is to violate his or her sovereignty, and habeas corpus has come to ensure that does not happen without proper cause.

. . .

Private property, Rule of Law, and individual sovereignty are three of the oldest principles of liberalism. Far from the popular caricatures of liberalism, these and other principles form the very foundation of the liberal philosophy that underlies our society, and each has played a crucial role in the establishment of America and our basic principles.

AMERICAN LIBERAL PRINCIPLES

Liberal principles reached a unique expression in America at the time of the Revolution. Much of the content of the Declaration of Independence, the Constitution, and the Bill of Rights was previously formulated, developed by colonial legislatures in constitutions, or otherwise emerged in the colonies before independence. These three documents bring together the unique expression of American liberal principles and to the thinking reader, they can leave no doubt that America is a liberal nation.

DECLARATION OF INDEPENDENCE

We hold these truths to be self-evident, that all men are created equal, that they are endowed by their Creator with certain unalienable rights, that among these are Life, Liberty, and the pursuit of Happiness. That to secure these rights, Governments are instituted among Men, deriving their just powers from the consent of the governed. That whenever any Form of Government becomes destructive of these ends, it is the Right of the People to alter or abolish it, and to institute new Government, laying its foundation on such principles and organizing its powers in such form, as to them shall seem most likely to effect their Safety and Happiness.

These words eloquently declare the unalienable rights of man, and are now understood to include every person. As a human being, each individual has the right to personal sovereignty, to not be violated in particular ways, and to live fully and completely in Life, Liberty, and the pursuit of Happiness.

The Declaration also states the purpose of government, which is to secure those rights. Any government failing in that duty can be altered or abolished, and replaced with something different.

The rest of the document lists complaints against the King of Great Britain. A careful reading of the Declaration indicates that the central concern of these complaints was the violation of sovereignty—the sovereignty of the colonies and the sovereignty of the individual. In the language of the Revolution such violations constitute tyranny. Here are a few examples enumerated:[25]

> The history of the present King of Great Britain is a history of repeated injuries and usurpations, all having in direct object the establishment of an absolute Tyranny over these States. To prove this, let Facts be submitted to a candid world....
>
> He has refused his Assent to Laws, the most wholesome and necessary for the public good ...
>
> He has obstructed the Administration of Justice, by refusing his Assent to Laws for establishing Judiciary powers.
>
> He has made Judges dependent on his Will alone, for the tenure of their offices, and the amount and payment of their salaries.
>
> He has erected a multitude of New Offices, and sent hither swarms of Officers to harass our People, and eat out their substance.
>
> He has kept among us, in time of peace, Standing Armies without the Consent of our legislature.
>
> He has affected to render the Military independent of and superior to the Civil Power....
>
> For protecting [armed troops], by a mock trial, from Punishment for any Murders which they should commit on the Inhabitants of these States:

---

25   Ellis, Joseph J. *What Did the Declaration Declare?* Bedford/St. Martin's, Boston–New York, 1999. Excerpts from the Declaration of Independence are taken from this source.

For depriving us, in many cases, of the benefits of Trial by Jury:

Tyranny refers to the autocratic domination of a person or country, i.e., the violation of sovereignty. Hence, the most basic liberal tenet of political consciousness is the notion that individuals should be free from tyranny. Although the Declaration was written against the King of Great Britain, the founding fathers had other tyrannies in mind as well. The original patriots guarded against excessive presidential power which could create the same tyrannies.

Tyranny is one of the most important words that occurs in the letters and other writings of America's founding fathers. They document three primary types of tyranny: the feudal-church power structures, privilege and its arbitrary discretion and enforcement, and the majority itself.

For over one thousand years, pre-modern power structures practiced tyranny throughout Europe—perhaps never so fiercely as in the two hundred years from the Reformation to the birth of America. At the time of the Declaration of Independence, the history of that period included horrific events such as the St. Bartholomew Day's massacre in France (1572), English campaigns of religious purification carried on through the reigns of King Edward VI (1547), Queen Mary (1553), and Queen Elizabeth (1558), periodic wars, uprisings, and skirmishes, and the constant persecution of one sect or another, depending on the religious preference and degree of tolerance of the king or queen in power. In America, the intolerance of the Salem witch trials was recent history. To Thomas Jefferson, Benjamin Franklin, and their contemporaries, such events were pointed reminders of what people can do to each other because of religious differences.

These displays of tyranny and abuses of power—in war, political repression, Inquisitional repression, intellectual repression—gave rise to political liberalism. Liberalism unseated the king in the popular imagination, as well as in political fact, by placing power firmly in the hands of the people. The Declaration of Independence is the declaration of this precise change in America, which is also expressed clearly in our Constitution, and in the way human and civil rights have grown and developed over two and a half centuries. Leaders are elected, but no elected leader has absolute power, for to have absolute power is to invite tyranny. The tyranny of Great Britain's king was uppermost in the minds of the founding fathers.

The privileged aristocracy practiced a second form of tyranny. The nobility and landowners took full advantage of their position. The social and cultural structure placed them as superior to the non-land-owning peasants. In contrast, liberalism removes the privilege conferred by birth through exerting control through the Rule of Law, opening opportunity to everyone. Society makes available to all citizens equal opportunity in public service, in the economy, in politics, in expression, in education, and in religion. Although America's expression of equal opportunity was not complete in the late 1700s—blacks and women were excluded—the seeds for development were sown and continued to germinate in the Emancipation Proclamation, women's suffrage, the Voting Rights Act, and the Civil Rights Act. America has by no means succeeded in eliminating privilege or its tyrannies, but from a historical perspective, the American spirit continues a commitment toward liberal ideals. Much of American history can be read as the gradual fulfillment of the liberal promises made in the Declaration of Independence.

Finally, there is the tyranny of the majority. As the founding fathers contemplated the establishment of a democracy—which is essential to liberalism—they envisioned the possibility of a tyranny of the majority. If all power were placed in the hands of the majority—whether political, religious, ethnic, or otherwise—there could be no freedom or liberty for minorities, except by the will of that majority. This kind of majority rule was unconscionable. If all power lies with a majority or a minority, the size of that group is irrelevant to those who hold beliefs and ideas contrary to it. Freedom and liberty can flourish only if the rights of all are protected, even as majorities make law as a matter of practicality. The real genius of American government rests in this balance. Our liberal democracy was established specifically to address this issue, as laid out in the Bill of Rights, the Constitution, the traditions of Congress, and the rulings of the courts.

The founding fathers' experience with the King, their knowledge of history, and their wariness about the future ensured that they address different forms of tyranny as they put together the Constitution and the Bill of Rights.

THE CONSTITUTION

The United States of America was the first country to incorporate liberal philosophy and principle into its structure and operation. Indeed, America was the first nation ever founded solely on written documents, in itself a victory for liberalism. Formerly, nations had been founded by the inspiration of a king, the initiation of the noble class, or religious negotiation or decree. The new America was the objective expression and documentation of principle. The form of the new nation precisely reflected its underlying principles.

Liberal consciousness further manifested itself in the mechanics of the new government. The three branches, checks and balances on power, elections, the electoral college, and even the process for amending the Constitution were all designed to prevent the concentration of power in one person or place. The mechanics of government provided the method for ongoing democracy, including how to change the government in response to changes in society. The Constitution is a hierarchy of ideas expressed as the mechanics of government. *Regulations*, promulgated and enforced by the *executive* branch, tend to lead change, and are therefore primarily *progressive* in nature, and deal with things which are easily changed. The *laws* of the land, passed by the *legislature*, reflect the will of the people and are *moderate* in nature. They reflect compromise between competing interests, viewpoints or positions. The *principles* of liberalism on which the nation is founded are guarded by the *judiciary*. This level of the hierarchy is inherently *conservative*, preserving our commitment to the principles of self-government, liberty, and freedom. Finally the most conservative aspect of all, the *philosophical* roots of the nation, are expressed in the *Constitution*. This level expresses the *dogma* of liberalism, and requires the assent of Congress, the president, and three-fourths of the state legislatures for amendment. Taken together, these constitute the political expression of the form of liberal consciousness.

Although the issues around the separation of powers are fairly well known, there is a fourth branch of the government is not handled directly: the people. The people are enfranchised through the vote, and the sanctity of the vote is essential to the integrity of self-government. Regardless of the other problems we may experience in our government, the sanctity of the vote is one of the most troubling issues of elections from 2000 through 2006. Auditable voting ought to be an obvious need in America, yet we've accepted electronic voting machines with no paper trails. Access to these machines cannot be tracked and they are wide open for voter fraud. How long will Americans wait to ensure that our one guaranteed way of speaking decisively is not taken from us by fraud? Without the integrity of the vote and the vote count, we lose the legitimacy of government.

In the Constitution, the separation of powers is a wall against tyranny, and its flexibility enables it to endure. The Constitution reflects the liberal, Enlightenment principles dominant in Revolutionary America, principles that have carried the dreams of the American people ever since. The document, the government, the nation, even the people are imperfect, but no better system has been devised for unleashing the creative, energized genius of a people.

BILL OF RIGHTS
The expression of America's liberal philosophy is found in the Bill of Rights, the critical first ten amendments to the Constitution. The Bill of Rights helped to broker and seal the deal between the states, wherein the rights of religious, political, and economic minorities, down to a single individual, are protected. Again, it is a matter of sovereignty. Rights such as freedom of expression and association, freedom to bear arms, freedom from unreasonable search and sei-

zure, and the right to privacy illustrate the premise. These rights protect the liberal freedoms that put power in the hands of each individual, rather than in the hands of a tyrant.

Many of the rights enumerated in the Bill of Rights have a long history in English law, Enlightenment thought, and the histories of the individual colonies. Habeas corpus provisions—which go back at least to 1500—appear in the amendments. The religious freedom provisions were central to Virginia's charter and were insisted upon by Jefferson, Madison, and Monroe, but also supported by early evangelicals who did not want to see a state religion supported by their tax dollars. The key provisions of the Bill of Rights came out of the worldview held by the founders. Liberal principle is part of a large, inevitable movement toward liberty for all.

Perhaps the most famous amendment of all is the First Amendment, which reads as follows:

> Congress shall make no law respecting an establishment of religion, or prohibiting the free exercise thereof; or abridging the freedom of speech, or of the press; or the right of the people peaceably to assemble, and to petition the government for a redress of grievances.

Separation of church and state, freedom of speech and the press, the right to protest: this amendment in particular is meant to keep the people involved in government. It enables us to gather, converse, think, and express ourselves freely because government of, by, and for the people requires such involvement. Alienate the people through religious or political ideology, and liberal democracy fails.

The Second Amendment is a bow to the states' right to have militias and the people's right to bear arms as a way of preventing tyranny against the people, based on the concept that an armed citizenry is an effective deterrent to government tyranny.

A well regulated militia, being necessary to the security of a free state, the right of the people to keep and bear arms, shall not be infringed.

The Fourth Amendment is a protection of individual sovereignty, ensuring that we cannot be searched or our property seized without just cause.

> The right of the people to be secure in their persons, houses, papers, and effects, against unreasonable searches and seizures, shall not be violated, and no warrants shall issue, but upon probable cause, supported by oath or affirmation, and particularly describing the place to be searched, and the persons or things to be seized.

If one reads the Bill of Rights next to the Declaration of Independence, it is easy to see that many of the amendments in the Bill of Rights are a direct response to the complaints leveled in the Declaration. This is significant because the two documents are separated by over twelve years. The issues covered in the two documents derive from enduring concerns of the founding fathers.

The Bill of Rights demonstrates how America started with a relatively limited, nascent application of these rights, and has slowly fulfilled them over the years. The Bill of Rights was originally designed to limit only the powers of the federal government—states could, and often did, establish policies which would later be seen as violations of civil liberties. This interpretation of the Bill of Rights was reinforced in an 1833 case, Barron v. Baltimore, by the Supreme Court. Chief Justice John Marshall, speaking for a unanimous Court, determined that the Bill of Rights applies to actions of the federal government, and not to those of the individual states.

After the Civil War, Congress passed the Fourteenth Amendment, whose first section—the so-called "due process and equal protection" clause—ought to have ensured that the rights of blacks in the south were not eliminated or infringed. It guaranteed that the rights and privileges of all citizens could not be abridged by the state governments. Beginning in 1920s, the Supreme Court began to affirm in several decisions that the first section of the Fourteenth Amendment did in fact mean the protections in the Bill of Rights applied to local and state governments as well as the federal government.

We have come to understand the Bill of Rights as the document which establishes the most basic rights of liberty for all Americans. It draws on the principles of liberalism discovered, elucidated, and worked out over hundreds of years before it was written, and then expanded and applied to all Americans over the ensuing centuries. This is how America has fulfilled its promise of liberty.

Although America remains a bastion of freedom, recent developments have eroded the perceptions of many Americans about the freedom of dissent. Terrorism and the 9/11 attacks are false rationalizations to subvert our most basic rights and freedoms. How are we free when the government is holding people in prisons without charging them and without providing access to appropriate legal help? What is the guarantee that such practices and powers won't be used against others? The benevolence of the attorney general? It is, and should be, of deep concern that people in political opposition to the current president are routinely barred from entering taxpayer-financed appearances of the president. Some have been arrested. With practices like these, fear, not freedom, is on the march—and our core values as a nation are being slowly eroded.

The ultimate test of our commitment to freedom of expression is in the freedom to express that which we find reprehensible. This point is made cogently in the film *The People vs. Larry Flynt*, directed by Czech filmmaker Milos Forman. In an interview several years ago, speaking from a historical context, he said that he made the film because Americans didn't understand the subtle ways in which fascism develops. As a young man, Forman watched fascism sprout its roots in Europe. The first stage was to articulate the evil of pornography. Almost everyone could be persuaded to hate pornography and pornographers. Fascist leaders developed a unity of thought through skillful rhetoric and propaganda. Who would disagree that society would be better if the pornographers were eliminated? Few, if any, would find a way to speak in favor of the pornographers.

Forman's insight and experience were that once the pornographers were widely understood as the demons of a society, people in power and the society itself began imperceptibly to expand the notion of what pornography is. His point was that while it starts with Larry Flynt—the publisher of *Hustler Magazine*—the parameters are insidiously expanded to nude art, contraception programs, sex education, and abortion clinics. As the process unfolds, any group can be demonized by affixing the label "pornographer." Although they seem ridiculous, new terms like religious pornographers—people who don't agree with the dominant religion—economic pornographers—unions and co-ops on the one hand, corporate robber-barons on the other—and political pornographers—anyone opposed to the ruling party—arise in the political-cultural lexicon. Forman's point is that it starts with the targeting of one easily marginalized group, especially one that creates fear in the general populace.

If this problem seems remote and distant, consider the way in which Senator Joseph McCarthy used the word "communist" in the 1950s. He branded everyone and everything he didn't like as "communist"; he got people black-listed and their livelihoods were destroyed. It succeeded because millions of Americans were afraid of communism, he learned the rhetoric, and he labeled people with this awful accusation. But it was all false. Is there any similarity to how Americans are slinging the term "terrorist" today? That term falsely justifies all types of hatred, loathing, and abuse. It falsely justifies holding people in detention simply because the president deems them terrorists. It falsely justifies abuse and secret detention centers. It falsely justifies the Patriot Act and all its problems, powers, and invasions. The term has also been adopted into the common lexicon: people speak of "economic" terrorism, "environmental" terrorism, and even "religious" terrorism. The term has spread without any official prodding or push—it is how we tend to disseminate highly charged, feared terms, as a way of emphasizing the point. As the diffusion of the term occurs, the whole political discussion changes as well.

How the nation treats accused pornographers, terrorists, rapists, communists, and other greatly-feared, much-hated groups is a test of our commitment to civil rights and the freedoms we enjoy. The point is not to support pornography, terrorism, or communism, but rather to understand how these terms acquire the power to demonize people by association, and then expand to influence thought and debate in the country.

THINGS TO REMEMBER

- Liberalism is based on principles, not values. Principles are enduring and objective; values are transient, individualized, and subjective.

- Private property is a liberal principle that unlocks wealth and capital, thereby creating economic opportunity and decentralizing political power.

- The Rule of Law is built on the basic concept of individual sovereignty and freedom, and is the key building block in self-rule via democracy. Security is based on Rule of Law.

- Liberal principles held dear by Americans are expressed in our founding documents:

- The Declaration of Independence expressed unalienable rights.

- The Bill of Rights expressed individual and minority rights.

- The Constitution expressed separation of powers and the power to vote.

There should be little if any debate about these principles. All Americans ought to cherish them as the basis of our freedom, our liberty and our way of life. Liberalism is contained in these and other principles, but it goes beyond them and affects our entire worldview.

CHAPTER 3

Liberal Worldview: It's Not Just Politics

Americans most commonly think of liberalism in a political context, but liberalism is much larger. Liberalism is a worldview that emanates from the very roots of modern consciousness, and affects our basic assumptions about religion, economics, and politics. The liberal worldview springs from a primal source in the human longing for freedom and dignity. The depth and scope of its effect means that liberalism cannot permanently be suppressed.

This chapter discusses three aspects of liberalism from a broad perspective. First, modernity and liberalism originate from the same philosophical root: the reliance on reason and the pre-eminent importance of individual experience. The foundation of liberalism appeared in the Renaissance, and the profound changes in human consciousness and philosophy that began to occur at that time altered the way people in the West perceived the world. Liberalism defines the new consciousness, which is our worldview.

Second, the Reformation arose from the collision of Christian religion with liberal philosophy and its modern differentiations. That collision gave rise to liberal and mainstream Protestant theology, Christian fundamentalism, and eventually to profound changes in the Catholic Church.

Third, capitalism is a liberal economic system that allows for optimal expression of economic freedom. When individuals make decisions about the deployment of capital and labor in a fair market, the result is an optimally creative economy. Unfortunately, capitalism has been distorted by structures foreign to its constitution, especially corporations. By the end of this chapter it should be clear that liberalism is far more than a left–wing political idea—it colors everything we do, see, and understand in modern America.

LIBERAL CONSCIOUSNESS

In his book, *A Theory of Everything*, Ken Wilber[26] puts forth a grand framework for studying and understanding the individual and collective aspects of the human being. The development of organisms, individuals, and societies generally moves toward higher levels of consciousness. Wilber demonstrates that there is wide, general agreement on this notion from scientists and researchers across most disciplines of study. But the development is not a straight line; it unfolds in *waves* or *lines*, and includes different states and types of consciousness.[27] Although development is a messy, fluid, overlapping, intermeshing affair, it is nonetheless real.

According to Wilber, the essence of the feudal, Middle–Ages type of consciousness is domination by powerful people, gods, and archetypes; empire, honor, and glory; the early sense of self as separate from the tribe, yet not fully differentiated; righteous order, rigid social hierarchy, and literal belief systems.[28] Material progress is won mostly by conquest.[29] Religious experience is mediated. Different aspects are stronger in different locations at different times, but the general trend of society and consciousness takes this form. Honor, order, duty, obedience, allegiance—these were the psychic currencies of feudal consciousness, and they went hand–in–hand with a feudal church–state partnership and the economy of con-

---

26 Wilber, Ken. *A Theory of Everything*. Shambala, Boston, 2000.

27 *Op. cit.*, p. 43. I owe the notion of unfolding waves of consciousness to Wilber.

28 *Op. cit.*, pp. 9–10.

29 Friedman, Benjamin. *The Moral Consequences of Economic Growth*. Alfred A. Knopf, New York, 2005.

quest. This medieval consciousness dominated the Western world throughout that historical period.

Using his model, Wilber argues that a major development occurred in Western consciousness with the Renaissance. Europeans began to differentiate aspects of being. For example, with the birth of modernity, art, morals, and science became differentiated.[30] Politics, economics, and religion separated into their own spheres. We began to see ourselves in the differentiated categories of state, self, and society.[31]

Renaissance philosopher René Descartes (1596–1650) laid the foundation of modern liberal philosophy: reliance on reason and the pre-eminent importance of individual experience—"I think, therefore I am." Although Descartes was overly mechanistic in his view of nature and the universe, these two ideas—reason and the individual—developed as pillars of modern liberal consciousness.

PSYCHOLOGICAL ROOTS

Pre-Modern	Modern
Righteous order	Individual reality
Codes of conduct	Rationalism
Honor-order-duty	Reason
Allegiance	Mechanistic universe
Conquest	Rule of law

Modern liberal consciousness developed an increased awareness of the self, and the individual's ability to know via experience. Thus, an individual's own experience and empirical sensibility became a more trusted guide to reality than the blind trust placed in king, clergy, or nobleman to dictate reality on the individual's behalf.

---

30   Wilber. *Marriage, op. cit.*

31   Stensland, Jonathan. Private conversation. Stensland has worked out an integrated modern view of this differentiation, many parts of which I draw on here and elsewhere in the book, to better understand liberalism as what he calls *ideology*, and what I have called *worldview*.

The Reformation was strongly influenced by this insight. Capitalism provided the economic basis of the individual's right to decide for himself, and liberal democracy enabled the individual expression of political will which would eventually overthrow the feudal system, the aristocracy, and later fascism and communism.

In the individual the new consciousness was fueled by the redis-covery of reason. Science and art moved forward with a focus on creativity, questioning, and searching. The self became more indi-vidual and less group-oriented—less loyal, dependent, and duti-ful, seeking expression in different ways; science and experience were found to be particularly adept at empowering such expres-sion. People trusted what they could see, study, and reason for themselves, rather than obediently accepting what they were told to believe. Natural laws could be learned, mastered, and manipulated. The original vanguard of the Renaissance flowed into the larger culture.[32] Out of it came a new way of thinking and perceiving the world—what I call *modern liberal consciousness.*

The new liberal consciousness became the basis for a new way of life, a new way of relating to the world, and a whole new set of chal-lenges, problems, and opportunities. Descartes, Newton, Coper-nicus, and other scientists changed our perception of the world. The dynamic interplay between society and consciousness created substantial changes for both. The religious, economic, and political structures were challenged strongly, as were the limits imposed on personal education, knowledge, creativity, and brilliance. Modern consciousness emerged as an engagement with reason, law, indi-vidual achievement, and self-authority—the very essence of liberal ideas and principles.

As the Enlightenment dawned in the seventeenth century, more and more people started thinking for themselves in the context, patterns, and differentiations of modern liberalism, even though it was not called liberalism at the time. Religion, economics, and pol-itics all went into crisis. Because the new ways of thinking changed our perception of reality, the wrenching challenges inherent in them

---

32   Wilber. *A Theory, op. cit.*

shook society to its foundations. Our minds changed, and along with them our assumptions about the world. Aristocrats, conquerors, kings, and clergy lost the near-universal acceptance of their positions. The old honor-order-duty consciousness was no longer legitimate and failed to deliver the same results as before. Hence, the psychological and philosophical changes of modernity complemented the structural changes in society.

THE DEVELOPMENT OF LIBERALISM

The early stage of liberal consciousness developed through the work of René Descartes, Francis Bacon, Martin Luther, and the early British capitalists. These leaders were scientific, rationalistic, and mechanistic in their approach. Philosophers, scientists, and other thinkers seriously contemplated the implications of these insights and ideas. First, they embraced the ideas developing out of science, such as Copernicus' sun-centered universe and Bacon's scientific method. These ideas greatly expanded human perception of the world. The world is a system, and by seeing it that way, we learned about it and how to manipulate it. But such thinkers also confronted the limitations of a rationalistic approach. Descartes' mechanistic systems, a major inspiration of liberal thought, would not be enough to understand the world. Early liberalism had its limitations, which its own reason exposed, and so by its own internal logic it was forced into a second stage of development.

The early liberal consciousness that viewed the world as a system can be overly intellectual. Systems look at inputs, outputs, and a process to reliably delivers results. But systems do not account for other, non-measurable phenomena such as feelings, intuitions, inspirations, and senses. The current spiritual crisis—to which fundamentalism and evangelicalism offer compelling but different answers—derives from this earlier stage of liberalism which American culture embraced for many decades. Likewise, intellectuals who followed the early thinkers confronted liberalism's limits, pushed new areas of exploration, and opened new realms of liberal consciousness.

Centuries later, the modes of understanding offered by Enlightenment science, materialism, and overly reductive thought processes confronted their limitations. Fueled by a new confrontation with the *humanity* of other races, Darwin's evolution, Einstein's relativity, and a globalizing economic order, new ideas gave rise once again to an expanded consciousness. This new consciousness embraced pluralism, diversity, and creativity. Evolution implied a human closeness to nature and animal instinct which Christian religion denied. Relativity suggested that little is absolute, space is curved, and much of what one understands depends on one's viewpoint. As much as we believe our own view to be "reality," others see things from a different vantage point, and therefore perceive a different reality. Ethnology and anthropology opened an understanding of the enormous variability of human cultures on the planet. The early liberal thought of Newton, Descartes, and Copernicus has been superseded by new insights derived from the liberal seeking for new knowledge. Not just a reaction, but a whole new creative leap occurred. It emerged in the late twentieth century as Gaia consciousness, non-linear thinking, and meditative practices which reflect higher orders of consciousness.[33]

As a result, this second stage of liberalism is more receptive to and adept at handling the new awareness of phenomena, knowledge, and experience. The complete experience of the individual is accepted in this framework, and thus enables an improved perspective on America's promise to optimize freedom. We must inquire about the realities faced by people, their perceptions, the reason for those perceptions, and how they affect people in general. Liberalism embraces these and many other questions that can foster a deeper, fuller understanding of human life, and a more vital experience of that life. American love of country is rooted in this idea, and it is profoundly liberal in nature.

---

33   Wilber, *op. cit.* See the sections and descriptions on the green meme. Some of these ideas are found there.

THE RELIGIOUS EXPRESSION OF LIBERAL CONSCIOUSNESS

For about one thousand years during the Middle Ages, Western society was dominated by the feudal-church partnership.[34] The religious component of this partnership was essentially Christian, and the Christian religious experience was mediated by the Roman Catholic Church or the Eastern Orthodox Church and its off-shoots. Christians experienced God through their clergy and clergy-mediated sacraments: mass, penance, marriage, and baptism. They prayed and worshipped by adhering to the structure and rules established by the church, absolved sins in confession, and received blessings through participation in communion. The church was always positioned between the people and their God so that the people got to God through the clergy. This structure also guaranteed the church's sole access to knowledge and its position of power within the society.

LIBERAL RELIGION

Pre-Modern	Modern
Church Hierarchy	Martin Luther
Mediated religious experience	Reformation
Honor-order-duty	Direct experience of God
Obedience	
Allegiance	

The Reformation was a direct challenge to this mediated experience and the authority structure it maintained. As part of the birth of liberal consciousness, Martin Luther posited the view that individuals could have a direct relationship with God, and therefore God could be experienced directly. Together with printing the Bible in the common languages of the people, this idea resulted in the new theological movement known as Protestantism. As literacy flour-

---

34   Lindsay, Thomas M. *A History of the Reformation*. New York, Charles Scribner's Sons, 1916.

ished, people could study the Bible directly for themselves without the interference of the clergy. The church's power eroded and the people were further empowered.

In Christianity, the idea of a direct experience of God developed in two ways. The first, more liberal, movement went beyond the questions of authority and knowledge, and encouraged followers to model one's individual life on Jesus.[35] Rather than following the rules of a mysterious and often manipulative clergy, worshippers modeled their lives on the morality of Jesus himself, who said, "Love your enemy," and "What you do to the weakest among you, you do unto me." Jesus rebelled against the rule-making power structure of the Pharisees, and he preached diversity, tolerance and love. "Let you who has not sinned cast the first stone." Christ provided an image to which to aspire, and liberal theology led the faithful in that direction. Worshippers were to model their lives on Jesus' example. Reading the story carefully, some have declared Jesus the greatest liberal of all time. A radical new unfolding of religious consciousness was at hand.

The second direction religion took tried to retain the old power relationships of the feudal-church structure. John Calvin led a major part of the Protestant movement to turn the "authority figure" of the feudal-church structure away from the church—with its priests, rituals, and hierarchical institutions—and place the authority in the Holy Bible alone. The Bible came to be viewed as the true Word of God. Because the Word of God is supposedly clear, the individual had little discretion in how he experienced God. God's Word, the direct experience of him, the moral code and how to behave are all stated obviously in the literal words of the Bible. The Bible amounts to God's commands to his followers. Known as Calvinism, revivalism, and Puritanism, this perspective has come to be known as fundamentalism. Fundamentalism is a way to destroy liberal theology using its own tools as much as possible. The liberal

---

35   Stensland, Jonathan. Private Conversation. Jonathan first pointed out this change in theological direction to me, and the notion was confirmed in other sources.

notion, "Decide for yourself," was replaced by the Puritan com-mand, "Read it for yourself." The freedom of liberalism was sacri-ficed to a new, impersonal authority, the comfort of "knowing" the truth, and a clear delineation of morality. Religious power accrued to those who quoted the Bible with the most authority, spoke the most loudly, and translated and printed the most Bibles. The essen-tial honor-order-duty structure of pre-modern consciousness remained unchanged in this response to modernity.

PROTESTANT REFORMATION
Authority in church

Authority in self	Authority in church	Authority in bible
Jesus as model	Mediated experience	Literal text
Conscience	Religious duty	Bible as God's word
Self-responsibility	Slow-moving reform movement	Honor-order-duty
Reason-Experience-Liberal Consciousness		Consciousness

This division into two directions, which occurred at the very birth of the Reformation, has defined a conflict in the religious expression of liberalism in America up to the present. For the most part, modern congregations accept Jesus' life as a model, and leave the interpretation and understanding of that up to the discipline and study of the individual. Right-wing congregations accept only biblical literalism as a way of knowing God; dissent is not accepted. Much of American political and cultural history tracks the rise and fall of these two religious forces, from the revivals and jeremiads of the right wing to the upsurges of Deism, Unitarianism, and the lib-eration theology traditions.

The third force, the Roman Catholic Church, resisted liberal change for centuries. Eventually the cultural force of liberalism led to profound changes in the church, the most significant being the reforms articulated in the early 1960s at the Second Vatican Coun-cil. The council restructured the Centuries-old order of the mass and replaced the traditional Latin with local languages. The changes promulgated at the Council also gave impetus to new movements: liberation theology in Latin America, peace and social justice ministries became active in many parishes, and lay ministers and nuns began to assist with the sacraments. In many ways the force of the human drive to freedom and individual liberty changed the church and finally brought it into the modern liberal age.

THE LIBERAL EXPRESSION OF RELIGIOUS FREEDOM

The liberal religious consciousness underlies the principle of religious freedom as expressed in the American Constitution. The founding fathers had three critical reasons to keep government out of church and church out of government. First, they were steeped in the Enlightenment ideas that came from Europe during the eighteenth century. Focused as they were on the differentiation of religion, economics, and politics, the separation of church and state was becoming an important principle. Second, they were aware of many recent atrocities and tyrannies committed in the name of religion during the time when Protestantism threatened to tear apart the Christian world. Unspeakable crimes against humanity were part of the recent historical record, most committed in the name of religion, and the founding fathers wanted to prevent such tyranny from occurring in the new nation. Finally, they had a pragmatic problem: the thirteen colonies were differentiated by radically different religious sects and radically different relationships between the state/colonial government and the dominant churches. There was no way to bind the colonies together with a single religious focus; to do so would cause an immediate fragmentation of the union. Keeping religion out of the federal government was the only possible way to bring such a government together.

The significant words of the First Amendment state the principle of separation of church and state, and together with the freedom of expression, guarantee all Americans the right to worship—or not—as they see fit. These words protect the church-goers from the non-church-goers, the Catholics from the Protestants, the Protestant mainline churches from the fundamentalists, the Jews from the Christians, the Christians from the Muslims. These words protect places of worship from government interference, and they protect the government from religion. The First Amendment protects the religious freedom and rights of everyone, and, in so doing, have prevented the kind of sectarian and religious wars that besiege so many other countries around the world. The right and freedom of everyone to worship as they see fit are protected under the American principle of separation of church and state.

Right-wing fundamentalists have long argued that the founding fathers meant to build a nation on their idea of God, and therefore, it was so obvious that they didn't need to mention God's name in the founding documents. This argument has forced the discussion onto the minutiae of the documents and biographies of the men, and away from the general liberal principles on which they stood. Such refocusing is a standard strategy of the fundamentalists because it enables them to rely on textual quotes, which is their strength given their literal study of the Bible. In this way, they avoid their weak spot, which is the honest engagement of discernment and thought. Robust debates and thoughtful writings on religion and government are part of the historical record. The establishment of state religion was considered *and rejected* for the very reason that it was, and is, so often used to justify tyranny. The freedom of religious expression is inextricably enmeshed in the separation of church and state and the unfolding of liberal consciousness. The Constitution, the Declaration of Independence, state charters, and state laws provide a history which amply illustrates the development of the principle that the state is secular—always secular. The state must always defend the rights of individuals and minorities against the possibility of majoritarian tyranny, and the area of religious expression is no exception. The vibrancy of America's religious community is the direct result of these freedoms. We need to recognize that the right-wing Christian attempts to breach this separation are attempts to express this very tyranny the founding fathers sought to avoid. Jefferson, Washington, Adams, and Franklin were civic geniuses; Jerry Falwell, Ralph Reed, and Pat Robertson are not.

The freedom of religious expression—even fundamentalist

religious expression—is a core principle of liberalism. All Americans enjoy this freedom, yet we are dangerously complacent about protecting it. This freedom is fundamental to being American, it is under attack from the Christian Right, and Americans have been ineffective in defending it, even though we cherish it. Religious freedom is under siege—the freedom to be Catholic, Protestant, agnostic, Jewish, Muslim, Hindu, atheist, deist, or whatever—and the freedom to express and live that faith in accordance with the authenticity of one's own convictions. No American wants to be forced to accept religious values that are contrary to his own perception, or to accept religion that conflicts with his own heart. Living honestly with our own values is part of the American ideal. We should not shrink from the fight to defend this ideal.

THE ECONOMIC EXPRESSION OF LIBERAL CONSCIOUSNESS

Under the tenets of economic liberalism, reason, stability, and sensitivity to the greater community allow individuals to engage their genius, bind together in small groups, and thrive by providing for the needs and desires of society. Each individual is as likely to encounter failure as success—there are no guarantees of outcomes—but it is the opportunity to engage one's own genius that lives at the heart of the liberal economy. Indeed, this is part of what the Declaration of Independence meant in referring to "the pursuit of Happiness."

The individualist roots of capitalism go back to the Enlightenment and to the Reformation. Adam Smith's *Wealth of Nations*[36] celebrates the benefits of capitalism as expressed in free markets and commerce. Benjamin Friedman, author of *The Moral Consequences of Economic Growth* (2005), outlines how Calvinist theology coming out of the Reformation urged individuals toward a fuller expression of individual economic wealth as the outward signs of inner grace.[37] Through this combination, individual action and religious belief

---

36 Smith, Adam. *An Inquiry into the Nature and Causes of The Wealth of Nations.* Edinburgh, 1776.

37 Friedman, *op. cit.*

become central to economic *and* religious practice, and the result is an honoring and celebration of the Christian entrepreneur.

American capitalism partially expressed this notion in the early history of the nation. It gave merchants, craftsmen, industrialists, and farmers the ability to seize economic opportunities as they saw fit, rather than limiting opportunity through the judgment of a Lord. This economic vision looms large in the American psyche; we call it The American Dream. It symbolizes the independence, the ability to engage one's own dream, one's own talent, and one's own value as the very heart of the creative economic dream. Capitalism is the freedom to engage your own discretion and the underlying belief that our system allows everyone that opportunity.

Although the economic philosophy of liberalism is capitalism, we should not confuse the *system* of capitalism with liberal economic *philosophy*. The system serves the dynamic creativity of the entrepreneur, from Carnegie and Rockefeller to Gates and Walton—and, more importantly, the millions of small- and medium-sized businesses developed by ordinary Americans. In serving such creativity, capitalism has raised standards of living and improved overall economic prosperity. But the system has also proved that it can be bent to serve those with feudal attitudes and ambitions. History has demonstrated this through the examples of the robber barons, monopolies, oligopolies, and large-corporation domination.

Fortunately, liberal economic consciousness is not so pliable. The American dream marches forward as inevitably as the drive for expanded consciousness has opened the human mind through the centuries. Capitalism works in service to this consciousness because it leaves the most critical economic decisions in the hands of the people who are free to choose how and where to deploy labor and capital. What is a worthy investment? What activity can add value? Individuals decide.

The term "private enterprise" expresses these principles in the area of human economic behavior. Liberal economics requires that free people allocate risk and reward according to merit and performance rather than privilege and position. The only two alternatives to liberal economics are feudal systems such as aristocracy, and nationalist totalitarian systems, which quickly collapse into crony-ism, or economics by position.

The liberal, private enterprise system enables resources and capital to be allocated according to the development of wealth as individuals and groups of individuals see fit. Individuals deter-mine what works for them. Such economics not only optimizes the fiscal independence of the individual—a core liberal value—but also protects political freedom by enabling individuals to legally obtain the tools essential to political expression, religious expression, and intellectual freedom. This freedom to decide the deployment of capital is deeply connected to the political freedom of expres-sion because without economic freedom, one cannot have access to printing presses, Internet servers, the electricity which runs them, or the paper on which to print political messages and ideas. The freedom to deploy capital also places economic control in the hands of the people who carry the economic consciousness.

Liberal economics illustrates the differences between conser-vative and progressive at least as much as liberal politics or religion. Conservatives in the liberal economic system often over-empha-size the individual. They tend to fully grasp the maneuverings and principles of creating and conserving wealth; this is their eco-nomic genius. Too often they succumb to the temptations of greed, or prefer methods of protecting position which are more akin to aristocracy than liberalism. Conservatives are also highly suscep-tible to a strain of arrogance which accompanies success, believing they alone are responsible for that success. When greed, arrogance and wealth converge, they often create a dangerous combination in an individual—one which pits them against employees, community responsibility, the environment, and government itself.

On the other hand, extreme progressives tend to take things too far beyond the liberal principle of equal *opportunity* toward a guar-antee of equal *outcomes*. Either through misunderstanding wealth creation or being deeply suspicious of it, progressives often crit-icize economic activity that is "merely for profit." The progressive point is that there are other important values in addition to profit and wealth—and they are right. Progressives demand a balance in human values, and recognize the conflicts between unbridled individualism and the legitimate interests of the community, whether neighborhood, city, state, nation, or world. But progressive commentary on profit betrays its suspicion. Progressivism sometimes exhibits a disdain for profit, which becomes a short critical step toward policies of governmental redistribution of wealth through high taxes, social programs, and over-regulation of economic activity. Such notions often raise fears of a move toward communism. To the extent that profit and wealth are excluded, or even demonized, and incentives eliminated, economic creativity and productivity lose their allure. The outcome of extreme policies of economic control can be seen in the Soviet Union and Communist China. Both systems of economic and political control failed. *Liberalization* led to the break-up of the Soviet Union as well as the current boom in China's economy.

In American economic liberalism, conservative and progressive forces are locked in a dynamic interchange. There is nothing to lament here; it is as it should be. Economic liberalism requires the creation of an economic *environment*, expressed as a specific set of principles and structures, focused to optimize the freedom of the individual and the overall economic function of society. Government passes the laws which regulate the freedom of action and expression between people, and thereby is actively engaged in the life of the nation. Government must ensure the uniform application of law, principles, and structures so that economic players may act with confidence that their efforts will not be usurped by the arbitrary actions of government. America's ability to inspire such confidence, together with the blessing of natural resources, puts us in a position of economic leadership. Challenges to that leadership exist only in those large countries restructuring their economies on liberal economic principles, reinforcing the notion that liberal economics is key for freedom and robust economic development.

THINGS TO REMEMBER

- Honor-order-duty consciousness dominated the Middle Ages, and liberal consciousness defines modern thinking. Regard for individual experience and reason are pillars of liberal consciousness.

- The Reformation, which gave us mainstream Protestantism as well as fundamentalism, was based on the liberal idea of authority residing in the self. Separation of church and state derives from the concept that no one can make an individual believe or appear to believe things that he or she does not find to be true. Even the Catholic church finally underwent dramatic changes due to liberalism.

- Capitalism is the liberal economic system that enables individuals to deploy labor and capital according to one's own discretion. Political and religious freedom require economic freedom in order to function.

Let us recall that liberalism is not one side of a liberal-conservative split in American politics. That idea serves only those forces opposed to liberal democracy. Rather, liberalism is a worldview that is comprehensive in its impact on the character and culture of America. Liberalism is based on old, widely-held philosophies and principles like private property, Rule of Law, and separation of powers. Further, the vibrancy of American liberalism depends on the contributions of three modalities: progressive, moderate, and conservative. American liberalism is, indeed, the overarching idea that binds us together as Americans.

To recall this is to beg a question: Who opposes this? What is there to be against? There are all too many people with different agendas—opponents who need to be repelled by people of good will. Identifying and repelling them is the subject of Section II.

Repel the Opponents

CHAPTER 4

The Allure of Theocratic Fascism

SINCE 1990, POLITICAL RHETORIC ON THE RIGHT AND THE LEFT have increasingly used the word "fascism" in an attempt to describe what they see or fear in political culture. Fringe groups and ideologues on both sides use the term easily, but only recently have government leaders like Secretary of Defense Donald Rumsfeld begun to use the term. His 2006 hyperbole equating fascism, Nazism, and Hitler to Osama bin Laden seem targeted to reinforce fear in the general population.[38] Maybe there is reason to fear, but one antidote to fear is knowledge. So before we look specifically at the events in America, I will introduce fascism through its twentieth century architect, Benito Mussolini.

Mussolini actually wrote an encyclopedia definition of fascism in 1932 in which he defined fascism as a philosophy: "Fascism is not only a system of government but also and above all a system of thought."[39] His idea was that the State was the vehicle through which all people would harness and connect to their own greatness, their destiny, their sense of being as a people. As a system of thought and philosophy, it was weighted toward intellectuals, and Mussolini,

---

38   Rumsfeld, Donald. Speech to American Legion, September 2006.

39   Available from multiple websites, including: http://www.fordham.edu/halsall/mod/mussolini-fascism.html, http://www.worldfuturefund.org/wffmaster/Reading/Germany/mussolini.htm, http://www.historyguide.org/europe/duce.html.

like Hitler, had his own intellectuals bending and creating scholarly thought to the will of the State and its view on morality, quality, and excellence.[40] Mussolini's sense of the State can be understood through these quotations from the encyclopedia entry:[41]

> The Fascist conception of the State is all embracing: outside of it no human or spiritual values can exist, much less have value. Thus understood, Fascism is totalitarian, and the Fascist State—a synthesis and a unit inclusive of all values, interprets, develops, and potentates the whole life of a people.
>
> The State, as conceived and realized by Fascism, is a spiritual and ethical entity for securing the political, juridical, and economic organization of the nation, an organization which in its origin and growth is a manifestation of the spirit.
>
> The Fascist State lays claim to rule in the economic field no less than in others; it makes its action felt throughout the length and breadth of the country by means of its corporative, social, and educational institutions, and all the political, economic, and spiritual forces of the nation organized in their respective associations, circulate within the State.

Mussolini's articulation of the doctrine goes on to claim a kind of spiritual purity for the fascists and deep disdain for liberalism. Repeatedly, he defiles liberalism and democracy as ideas and methods of government which reduce the State to the lowest common denominator.

---

40   See Pringle, Heather. *The Master Plan: Himmler's Scholars and the Holocaust*. New York, Hyperion, 2006.

41   Available from multiple websites, including: http://www.fordham.edu/halsall/ mod/mussolini-fascism.html, http://www.worldfuturefund.org/wffmaster/ Reading/Germany/mussolini.htm, http://www.historyguide.org/europe/duce. html.

Fascism trains its guns on the whole block of democratic ideologies, and rejects both their premises and their practical applications and implements ... it asserts the irremediable and fertile beneficent inequality of men who cannot be leveled by any such mechanical and extrinsic device as universal suffrage.

Fascism is definitely and absolutely opposed to the doctrines of liberalism, both in the political and the economic sphere.

Under fascism, the state is the authoritarian arbiter of quality, excellence, integration, and morality:

To achieve this purpose it enforces discipline and uses authority, entering into the soul and ruling with undisputed sway.

No action is exempt from moral judgment: no activity can be despoiled of the value which a moral purpose confers on all things.

Putting it together, Mussolini offers this summation:

The Fascist State, as a higher and more powerful expression of personality, is a force, but a spiritual one. It sums up all the manifestations of the moral and intellectual life of man. Its functions cannot therefore be limited to those of enforcing order and keeping peace, as the liberal doctrine had it. It is no mere mechanical device for defining the sphere within which the individual may duly exercise his supposed right. The Fascist State is an inwardly accepted standard and rule of conduct, a discipline of the whole person; it permeates the will no less that the intellect. It stands for a principle which becomes the central motive of man as a member of society, sinking deep down into his personality; it dwells in the heart of the man of action and of the thinker, of the artist, and of the man of science; soul of the soul.

To Mussolini and Hitler, the State was the supreme determinant of morality, wisdom, spirit, wealth, knowledge, and power. The people were to follow the state, rather than the state being formed as an instrument of the people to govern themselves. With these notions in mind, we can consider the American temptation with theocratic fascism.

SEEING THE THREAT

Theocratic fascism is a kind of totalitarian government that bases its policies and dictates partly on theological grounds, partly on philosophical grounds, and partly on the maintenance of its own power and position. In America, fundamentalist Christianity supplies the theological foundation; the underlying philosophy comes from the political philosophy of neoconservatism; and the power structures are woven into corporate bureaucracies, supported by corporate cultures, and maintained by unprecedented cronyism and greed. When these factors come together, their combined power is substantial—enough so that they currently control all three branches of the federal government.

To understand the nature of the threat posed by the right wing, we must first understand how totalitarian fascism develops. Friedrich A. Hayek was a member of the Austrian School of Economics, a Nobel Laureate, and the author of several books. Writing in the last year of World War II, Hayek warned Western countries of the ways in which socialism and the ideals which serve it can combine with nationalism to lead whole nations into totalitarian nightmares. Hayek traced the development of fascism from its roots in socialist and nationalist political theory. At the time, he was most concerned about a perceived increase in the intellectual and political acceptance of socialist ideas in America and Europe, and what that would mean for the acceptance of totalitarianism. His work details the scale and scope of societal and cultural changes that occur over a several-decades run-up to a totalitarian regime.[42]

Sixty years later, Hayek is still valued by conservatives for his warning about socialism. The irony is that the conditions leading to socialism, communism, and fascism are the same. Even though communism and fascism are very different ideologies, the clarity of Hayek's insight enables us to identify and understand changes in our national political dialogue since the 1960s which have created conditions conducive to fascism. Our concern is not movement to the left or the right, but rather away from modern liberalism. The conditions for fascism are increasingly present right here in America.

Hayek outlines six factors which are necessary for the rise of totalitarian control:

1. The articulation of a central organizing philosophy based on the common good and "Ideal Society".

2. The distortion of thought and ideation toward the Ideal Society vision.

3. The loss of real communication between the people—words lose their meaning through relentless propaganda.

4. The rise of the most ruthless to the top.

5. The bold, clear, harsh, public handling of dissent, and the absolute refusal to tolerate dissent.

6. The willingness of the people to trade freedom for security.

When Hayek wrote in 1944, his principal concern was the slide into fascism that led to World War II, and the tempting, powerful ideas of socialism that led to the totalitarian regime in the Soviet Union. He saw the utopian vision of the socialists and fascists and

---

42   In Hayek's day, the rise of socialism, fascism, and totalitarianism was a major concern. Hayek was most concerned about the influence of socialists in America and England—and the possibility of similar results. To read Hayek today for the influence of socialism would be a mistake. Rather, his contribution is to the understanding of the forces at work when totalitarianism has found fertile ground in a given society, as outlined in his conditions above.

how intellectuals distorted their thought to fit the vision. He bore witness to the destruction of meaningful language and conversation through propaganda and spin. Hitler, Stalin, and Mussolini were present in people's memories when Hayek wrote of the "ruthless" who rise to the top. All totalitarian governments treat harshly those who dissent. The "security" people chose over freedom was economic security, hence Hayek's focus on socialist visions.

All of these factors are present in American society today, an ominous and dangerous development. The conditions for fascism at home are met in the unity of Christian fundamentalism, neoconservatism, and the corporate power elite. We must understand the basic motivations and ideas of each and open our eyes to the reality of the consequences, whether deliberate or not.

CHRISTIAN FUNDAMENTALISM

The clearest, most notable vision of the "ideal" society driving politics in America today is the ideology of the Christian Right. Although fundamentalism has been with us for a long time,[43] the articulation of this ideal in its recent form started on a large scale with the formation of the Moral Majority in 1979. Jerry Falwell's group—and fundamentalist Christians throughout the country—clearly articulated their vision of an ideal society. It would be a righteous society of Christian, God-fearing people, in which God is revered, incorporated into our laws, and built into our public institutions. Literal reading of the Bible inspires the law of the land. Christian legislators create Christian laws, enforced by a Christian executive and adjudicated by Christian judges, all of whom shepherd a Christian people guided by a Christian clergy.

If you doubt the comprehensiveness of this vision, here is

---

43   Armstrong, Karen. Speech, Westminster Town Hall Forum, Minneapolis, 2005.

George Grant, a fundamentalist leader, stating the goal in his book *The Changing of the Guard: Biblical Principles for Political Action*:[44]

> Christians have an objective, a commission, a holy responsibility to reclaim the land for Jesus Christ—to have dominion in civil structures, just as in every other aspect of life and godliness. But it is dominion we are after. Not just a voice. It is dominion we are after. Not just influence. It is dominion we are after. Not just equal time. It is dominion we are after. World conquest. That's what Christ has commissioned us to accomplish. We must win the world with the power of the Gospel. And we must never settle for anything less.... Thus, Christian politics has as its primary intent the conquest of the land—of men, families, institutions, bureaucracies, courts and governments for the Kingdom of Christ.

This is no ordinary Christianity. It is a literal, fundamentalist brand that seeks dominion and comes straight out of the honor-order-duty consciousness of pre-modern times. Such consciousness appeals to masses of people and has given rise to many similar organizations, from TV evangelists to the Christian Coalition. All these groups articulate the vision of an ideal society in God's image. Totally committed to their faith, these groups have organized and developed to exercise a new strength in American politics. Like the European nationalist-fascist movement of the early twentieth century, this theocratic movement has developed its influence and systematically gained control of large parts of our political system over a twenty-five-year period.

The Christian fundamentalists not only have strong political action committees and congregation-level organization, but a legal foundation to pursue litigation in their favor. They have cre-

---

44 Grant, George. *The Changing of the Guard: Biblical Principles for Political Action*. Middlesex, Dominion Press, 1987, pp. 50–51.

ated Christian law schools, like Regents University,[45] whose goal it is to graduate attorneys—who will become judges—trained to believe that "God's law" is of equal weight with U.S. law.[46] Other Christian schools focus on preparing, justifying, and graduating CIA agents and career professionals who hold Pat Robertson's belief that assassination of foreign leaders is a legitimate option in American foreign policy. Through this vision of the God-oriented society, Christian fundamentalism has co-opted the political allegiance of many people under the rubric of its theology.

Fundamentalist Christian evangelists lead prospective converts to believe that they are not quite real Christians until they become born again, thereby implying that mainstream Christians like Episcopalians, Lutherans, and Roman Catholics are not legitimate. Why? A central idea underlying fundamentalism is that most Christians are not really Christians because they cannot identify the day and time when they "accepted Jesus Christ as their savior." Hayek describes what happens in the culture of nations tending toward totalitarianism:

> The people are made to transfer their allegiance from the old gods to the new under the pretense that the new gods really are what their sound instinct had always told them but what before they had only dimly seen.[47]

Fundamentalists convert other Christians to their way of seeing

---

45   In a clear declaration of purpose, the Regents University Law School uses this quote on their web page: "Regent University School of Law is distinctive among law schools approved by the American Bar Association because of the integration of Christian Principles into our curriculum. It is this balance of professional legal training and the affirmation of biblical principles that enables our graduates to provide excellent legal counsel to their clients." http://www.regent.edu/acad/schlaw/welcome/facts.cfm.

46   Hagerty, Barbara Bradley. "Religious Schools Train Lawyers for Culture Wars," report for NPR, May 6, 2005.

47   Hayek. *Op. cit.*

the world, and those who convert inevitably feel "more Christian" than they did before. Conversion feels good because life after conversion is simpler; there are now answers to all life's complexities. In other words, converts are now in alignment with "what before they had only dimly seen." Theologically, one comes into the light only upon acceptance of Jesus Christ as one's personal savior, a definition formulated by the fundamentalists themselves.

The convert who accepts Christ in the prescribed manner adopts a whole new vocabulary and thought process. A new vision of a morally ideal—and superior—society develops, a vision apparent to anyone who reads the Bible literally. Because the Bible is taken to be the actual Word of God, what true Christian could dissent? To question is to sin and incur the wrath of God and God's soldiers and witnesses. In this way, theological obedience yields a political force perfectly pliable under the direction of its ostensibly theological leaders.

The pliability of worshippers is developed in two ways: first, a militaristic sense of duty to do "God's will." The Christian fundamentalist's *duty* is to help God create his ideal society by "witnessing to others" and improving society through political action. "That's what Christ has commissioned us to accomplish," George Grant wrote. People simply follow and do what the church leadership decrees is necessary to God's vision. As the interpretation of that vision becomes increasingly politicized, this dynamic creates an electoral subgroup easily manipulated by its leaders. The stern ruthlessness of a man like George Grant, is either overlooked passively or actively celebrated as an indication of superior commitment to God.

Second, an extreme level of intellectual isolation—which results from the narrow reading of the Bible and the isolation of church communities—becomes central to Christian fundamentalist life. The sense of duty to God leads people to focus on biblical interpretations of *everything*. No authority challenges literal interpretations of the Bible. Even the slightest internal dissent is considered by the church community as a sin against God. The *literalization* of the truth manifests itself individually as a loss of critical thinking and vital, original, real experience; it manifests itself socially as religious fundamentalism and political totalitarianism.

As a critical result, communication with other viewpoints completely breaks down, as Hayek indicated it does on the road to totalitarianism. There can be little or no reasoned discourse with a fundamentalist because, by definition, the fundamentalist already has all of God's answers; they are in the Bible for anyone to read. His certainty means there is no need to entertain the questions. To any question, he will answer, "Well, the Bible says ..." To him, the literal Bible is the ultimate source of knowledge for the law, for morality, for everything. Fundamentalists have learned that this way of thinking is not attractive to the general public, so they have developed a clever way of responding: the right-wing churches, Christian schools, and summer camps now teach Christian fundamentalists how to convey their ideas in more acceptable terms, while preserving the underlying thought process and energy of their evangelism.

We see this in our schools today in the fight over the Christian rejection of evolution as a scientific theory, and the effort to replace it with "intelligent design." Intelligent design, a euphemism for creationism, is a doctrine that is congruent with the literal interpretation of the Bible. Literal reading of holy books always fuels collisions between science and religion because science and fact rarely bear out the supposed literal truth of the texts. Such conflicts bring into question the entire edifice of literal-based faith, and hence, believers become very resistant to science that contradicts their beliefs.

Christian fundamentalist groups have also tried to change the history curriculum to suggest that the founding fathers were really born-again Christians. The founding fathers were so pious, this argument goes, they did not need to mention God in the founding documents because it was too obvious to mention. The historical record shows, however, that the dominant religious attitude of the founding fathers was Deism, the belief that there may be a God, but God's nature is not knowable in any meaningful way. The founding fathers actively debated and explicitly affirmed their commitment to church-state separation—the liberal principle that allows everyone the opportunity to interpret spirituality and religion for themselves. In fact, in several of the original colonies, evangelicals were the strongest champions of the church–state separation, while most Americans did not even attend church. Robert T. Handy, an historian of early American religion, says that only 10 percent of Americans were members of churches in 1800.[48] And yet, the right–wing Christian fundamentalist propaganda machine publishes textbooks, elementary school video tapes, web sites, and exams teaching that the framers were Christians, and, apparently, Christian fundamentalists. It is a deliberate effort to limit the intellectual range of study and indoctrinate children.

These examples illustrate how the Christian Right is using its so–called *values* to attack liberal *principles*. They do this because they cannot win a battle of principle against principle. The sole principle of the Christian Right—the literal truth of the Bible—cannot compete with liberal principles like liberty, reason, individual sovereignty, and religious freedom, and they know it. So the Christian Right attacks on the basis of values, refuses to engage the real argument, and confuses any rational discussion of the issue. Instead, they make an emotional appeal to irrational fears, establish a vast propaganda infrastructure, attack and discredit individuals who disagree, and constantly chip away at the liberal foundations of the nation. An electorate insufficiently educated in liberal principle is eventually swayed.

In these ways, the Christian fundamentalists contribute to Hayek's preconditions for totalitarianism. They present a vision of society which they claim to be for the common good. They actively distort thought and reality to bend it to their view of the world. They cut out the heart of good communications by cutting out the heart of honest communication based on real questions. And they make dissent from their ideas intolerable while ruthlessly demonizing the dissenters. The Christian fundamentalists are not enough by themselves to tip the nation into totalitarianism, but they are integral to

---

48 Handy, Robert T. *A History of the Churches in the United States and Canada*. Oxford University Press, Oxford–New York–Toronto–Melbourne, 1976, p. 162.

creating the new conditions that are leading the nation to the precipice. They need their powerful allies—the neoconservatives and the corrupt corporate elite—in order to accomplish that goal.

NEOCONSERVATISM

Who are the neoconservatives and what do they want? These two questions cause endless confusion and misunderstanding. Neoconservatives differ greatly from the Christian fundamentalists, although their policies and concerns are often complementary to those of the fundamentalists. Nor are the neoconservatives identical with the corporate elite, although their interests often overlap as well. These overlapping complementarities lead us to confuse the labels and use them interchangeably. This is a mistake. The neoconservatives have their own ideas, their own concerns, and their own agenda.

The lack of clarity is compounded by the changing ideas and sometimes foggy statements neoconservatism uses to try to define itself. It has no unifying statement, and people regularly move into and out of the ranks of neoconservatives. If one thing can accurately be said about neoconservatism it is this: neoconservatism is an *intellectual* movement. It started in academic circles, is deeply influenced by certain intellectuals in many areas of study, and continues largely as an intellectual movement with involvement in national policy.

Who are the neoconservatives? People like Irving Kristol and Daniel Patrick Moynihan were among the earliest. Paul Wolfowitz, Richard Pearle, Dick Cheney, Donald Rumsfeld, Alan Bloom, Francis Fukuyama, and Norman Podhoretz led neoconservatism through the 1970s and into the 1990s. At present, new leaders like Robert Kagan and William Kristol have emerged. Some of the names are recognizable, others are known primarily among intellectuals. But all shared the intellectual pursuit of neoconservatism at one time or another.

Some have identified the origin of the neoconservative movement in the mid-1960s with the appearance of *The Public Interest*, a new journal that joined the older and more well-known *Commentary*, to become one of the two flagship journals of the movement. Others insist that the movement didn't really start until the 1970s, while others trace it back to a professor named Leo Strauss, who taught at the University of Chicago starting in the 1930s. But with roots in publications and universities, there is no mistaking its intellectual base. It makes sense that "think tanks," designed to develop and advocate their ideas, are the preferred structure supporting the neoconservatives today.

Neoconservatism is hard to pin down because both the movement and the neoconservatives themselves change over time. Irving Kristol, the clear leader of neoconservatism in the 1970s, once defined neoconservatives as liberals who've been "mugged by reality," thereby suggesting the shift in attitudes many neoconservatives experienced. Kristol himself had been a Trotskyite in college, an avowed, left-leaning liberal for years after that, and eventually became editor of *Commentary*. A rigorous intellectual writer with a strong academic résumé, Kristol raised questions and issues that were outside the mainstream thought of the times.

Similar left-leaning origins appear in the biographies of many neoconservatives, and in some ways justify the prefix "neo" on neoconservative. They were "new" conservatives, people who moved to that view after having been "liberals." This shift characterized many of the first generation of neoconservatives, while the following generation of William Kristol—Irving's son—and Robert Kagan experienced no such youthful confusion, thereby eliminating the need for an "enlightened change."[49]

For the most part, attempts to define a neoconservative doctrine or platform have failed because of the changing nature of the positions held by individual neoconservatives, and because the positions being championed by its leading intellectuals have changed over time. In 1979, Peter Steinfels, then executive editor of *Commonweal*,

---

49   Max Boot. "Myths about Neoconservatism," in *The Neocon Reader*. Ed. Irwin Stelzer. Grove Press, New York , 2004.

made the first serious attempt to define this movement clearly—its ideas, its leaders, and its goals. Reviewing the extensive writings of neoconservative intellectuals, Steinfels deduced the following set of common philosophical assumptions held by neoconservatives:[50]

1. Neoconservatism holds that a crisis of authority has overtaken America and the West generally. Governing institutions have lost their legitimacy; the confidence of leading elites has been sapped. Social stability and the legacy of liberal civilization are threatened.[51]

2. The current crisis is primarily a cultural crisis, a matter of values, morals, and manners. Though this crisis has causes and consequences on the level of socioeconomic structures, neo-conservatism, unlike the Left, tends to think these have performed well. The problem is that our convictions have gone slack, our morals loose, our manners corrupt.[52]

3. Government is the victim of 'overload.' Attempting too much, it has naturally failed and thereby undermined its own authority.[53]

4. In the face of this crisis, neoconservatism insists that authority must be reasserted and government protected.[54]

5. A precarious international order requires a stable, unified society at home; renewed emphasis on the Communist threat and on the Third World's rejection of liberal values is needed to generate the requisite national allegiance and discipline.[55]

These five elements of neoconservatism help to define its agenda. Starting in the mid-1960s these elements can be read in

50   Steinfels, Peter. *The Neoconservatives*. Simon & Schuster, New York, 1979. pp. 53–67.
51   *Ibid.*, p. 53.
52   *Ibid.*, p. 55.
53   *Ibid.*, p. 58.
54   *Ibid.*, p. 63.
55   *Ibid.*, p. 67.

nearly everything written by neoconservatives. They help us identify neoconservatism's affinity with the Christian fundamentalists—
in the observation of moral decay and the insistence on a return to
strong morality—and its affinity with the free market capitalists and
power elite to fight for deregulation. One can also see the philosophical roots of the current president's assertion of presidential
authority. In fact, the alignment of Steinfel's analysis with the neoconservative outcomes of our current political situation is so striking as to tempt one to believe it was written as an interpretation of
our recent history and the current administration. It is sobering to
realize these philosophical tenets were deduced and articulated by
Steinfels in 1979, even before Ronald Reagan was elected president.

The five elements deduced and clarified by Steinfels bring
neoconservative motivations into focus. If the nation is in crisis
because the elite have lost confidence, the neoconservative remedy
is to win back the confidence of those leaders. But the leaders the
neoconservatives are concerned with are their friends in the corporate sector, their own intellectual brethren and the fundamentalist Christian leadership. Naturally, the neoconservatives champion
policies to favor these groups.

If we face a crisis of values, morals, and manners, the neoconservative strategy is to impose values, morals, and manners on the
country. Neoconservatives proved their willingness by supporting
right-wing positions on issues like Terri Schaivo, sex education,
war, and abortion. Far exceeding the obnoxious self-righteousness
of projects like Bill Bennett's *Book of Virtues*,[56] the legal and policy
maneuvers attempt to legislate individual morality for everyone.
As elites, the neoconservatives consider themselves better able to
determine the moral behavior of the people than the people themselves, so they claim justification for establishing a government that
determines what is moral and what is not. Placing that power in the
hands of government contradicts Rule of Law—one of the founda-

---

56 *The Book of Virtues*. Ed. William Bennett. Simon & Schuster, New York, 1993.

tional principles of liberalism—and has distinct echoes with Mussolini's definition of fascism.

The anti-government stance of neoconservatives derives from their sense of the ineffectiveness of government. From their perspective, government never tries to do too much in terms of military dominance and the expression of power, while government overreaches when it seeks to maintain liberal rule structures and ensure equality of opportunity. As a result, neoconservative calls for less government and more controlled spending lack credibility because their policies lead to monumental debt and enormous military spending and activity. In fact, such calls appear to be covering a less obvious agenda which is largely responsible for what many see as an imperial and fiscally reckless in America.

Neoconservatives champion a strong central authority in the executive branch of government. The policies of the Bush administration embody this goal and consistently concentrate power—discretionary power—in the presidency. Such concentration erodes basic principles of American liberalism.

Finally, neoconservatives seem addicted to wielding power. Power fascinates them, and they will seek to express it fully. As an example, the doctrine of tactical use of nuclear weapons goes back to 2000 at least, and has reappeared in the administration's strategic plans to handle the crisis with Iran.[57] Neoconservative foreign policy writings focus on the projection of American power oversees, and too often, as in the cases of both Iran and Iraq, arrogantly inflate the potential accomplishments of such power.

Remarkably, during the first six years of the Bush administration, the neoconservatives enjoyed a great deal of impunity in implementing their agenda: move power, money, and resources to the elite; impose moral values wherever possible; strengthen the authority of the president in order to better apply the agenda; and

---

57   Hersch, Seymour M. "The Iran Plans: Would President Bush Go to War to Stop Iran from Getting the Bomb?" *New Yorker*, April 17, 2006. http://www.newyorker.com/fact/content/articles/060417fa_fact.

extend American power into new regions based on a new, revised military. The effectiveness of the implementation is breathtaking.

A special document put together by the Project for the New American Century (PNAC)—a neoconservative think tank—has caused many Americans to sound the alarm. The report, published in 2000, *Rebuilding America's Defenses: Strategy, Forces and Resources For a New Century*,[58] is the blueprint used by the neoconservatives in power today. Who were its signatories?

Elliot Abrams	Donald Kagan
Gary Bauer	Zalmay Khalilzad
William J. Bennett	Lewis Libby
Jeb Bush	Norman Podhoretz
Dick Cheney	Dan Quayle
Eliot A. Cohen	Peter W. Rodman
Midge Decter	Stephen P. Rosen
Paula Dobriansky	Henry S. Rowen
Steve Forbes	Donald Rumsfeld
Aaron Friedberg	Vin Weber
Francis Fukuyama	George Weigel
Frank Gaffney	Paul Wolfowitz
Fred C. Ikle	

Some are intellectuals, such as Fukuyama and Podhoretz. Others are Christian fundamentalist leaders like Gary Bauer. Others are current and former administration officials:

Dick Cheney—Vice President
Donald Rumsfeld—Secretary of Defense
Paul Wolfowitz—Former Assistant Secretary of Defense
Zalmay Khalilzad—U.S. Ambassador to Iraq
Lewis Libby—Former Chief of Staff to Vice President Cheney

The reader will also notice other familiar names: Jeb Bush, the

---

58   A Report of the Project for the New American Century. Washington, DC, 2000.

president's brother and governor of Florida; Dan Quayle, former vice president under the current president's father; and Steve Forbes, presidential candidate and millionaire owner of *Forbes Magazine*.

That such people would get together to write a report and pool their ideas is not in itself alarming; what is alarming is the very radical agenda they proposed, and its implementation ever since the group came to power. The report is a blueprint for Bush administration policies: huge increases in military spending, the assertion of military power to create regime change and usher in democracy, control of global oil supplies, and the notion of American exceptionalism—the theory that we can create global rules but we need not follow them—are all clearly stated in the text of the document.

The PNAC report illustrates the breadth and depth of the neoconservative movement. The report clearly lays out the premeditated goal of attacking Iraq. When the goal is to establish bases in the Middle East and Persian Gulf regions and to topple unfriendly regimes, they show no compunction in doing whatever is necessary to carry out that goal: distort intelligence; deceive the American people; link Iraq to terrorism, however spuriously; and engage unilateral pre-emptive war. When the goal is to control the nation's morals, they pull out all the stops: pass a law applying to one person and fly the president to Washington from his vacation to sign the law, or threaten the "nuclear option" to get extremist judges approved by the Senate for the federal bench and the Supreme Court. Claim the authority—legitimately or not—to re-interpret the laws, write legal memos and "findings" that put the power in the president's hands. Claim executive power again and again.

The point is that the assertion of power, the flaunting of Rule of Law, the deception of the American people, and the attempt to legislate morality via state power all fulfill conditions which Hayek identified would be necessary for fascism. Fascist intellectuals posited frameworks for understanding the world in their terms in fascist Europe; the similarity to neoconservative intellectualism and Christian fundamentalist pseudo-intellectualism should make us pause. Neither the Christian fundamentalists or the neoconserva-

tives could accomplish much alone, however. They need their partners, the corrupt segment of the corporate elite.

CORPORATE POWER ELITE

Although Christian fundamentalists and neoconservatives provide
the primary philosophical drivers behind the right-wing movement in America, neither could stand without the third leg of the
stool: the participation of certain corporate elites, particularly those
willing to wield their power and resources to bend national interests toward their own. These are the *corrupt* corporate elite; many
corporate leaders are not corrupt. All corporate leaders have the
unique advantage of focus. Corporations enable and demand exclusive focus as no other organizational structure does. Hence, the
energy of corporate ideas concentrates on the use, development,
and expression of power, growth, and wealth. The corrupt corporate elite are indispensable to the right-wing movement because
they supply the raw power—and are rewarded with more. Corrupt corporate power has been utilized to extract wealth and control from the political sphere. Because corporations so effectively
concentrate economic power, they profoundly affect the political
landscape. Recognizing that an emerging influence—based on the
philosophical ideas perpetuated by neoconservatism and Christian
fundamentalism—serves their own organizational interests in direct
and important ways, such corporations are almost bound to support and enhance those ideas in whatever way they can. Under the
spell of the right wing, government gave corporations useful tools
and liberties—deregulation, subsidies, tax breaks, and lax enforcement—and corporations are using those tools to advance the ideas,
principles, and philosophies that cater to their own narrow interests.

The ideology of the corrupt corporate elite, energized by the
drive for money and power, reinforces itself by focusing on money
and power. So those who excel in the world of power and money
often rise to become the corporate power elite. Through the lens of
the corrupt corporate power elite, government is one of two things:

an obstinate regulator and obstruction to progress; or a gigantic piggy bank to break and rob. This segment of the corporate elite favors any political approach that can eliminate the obstruction or provide access to the piggy bank.

The great euphemism for the movement of money and power is "efficiency." Efficiency improves dramatically when the tenets and philosophies of neoconservatism and Christian fundamentalism are in place. While democracy is usually messy and untidy, it tends toward liberal principles and justice. In contrast, fascism is tremendously efficient, especially for deploying national resources in the hands of an elite few for whatever purpose they may decide. Particularly in this area, the philosophies of the corporate elite and the neoconservatives overlap and nicely complement one another. For example, complete and unfettered presidential authority provides the political structures neoconservatives favor, the moral center the Christian fundamentalists seek, and it is tremendously efficient in terms of getting things done. Appeal to the president, and he decides. But it means currying the president's favor in other ways, and that is where a direct relationship with campaign finance arises.

The corporate elite connect to the other legs of the right-wing movement primarily through campaign finance. The corrosive effects of the relationships are plain to all who care to look.[59] Elected officials stand at the hub of the relationship; their parties and their supporting organizations receive financial support to retain office and power, while in their turn the officials promote policies targeted to benefit the corporate elite. Tax cuts for the super wealthy, corporate welfare programs, and outsourcing functions of government to private entities are part of this relationship from which the elites benefit. The same benefit also shows up in legislation which purposely transfers powers to the corporations: The telecommunica-

---

59   The tacit relationship was first made clear in 1989 after Reagan left office and his well-heeled supporters gave him a $20 million ranch on which to live. Corporate influence has by no means been limited to the Bush administration, but is achieving new ascendancy here.

tions act of 1996, the bankruptcy bill, the Medicare drug benefit, NAFTA, CAFTA, and the awarding of no-bid contracts to privileged companies like Halliburton, are all recent examples of favoritism and power give-aways from government to corporations and their affiliates.

This relationship results in the de facto monopolization or nationalization of certain industries and businesses. Halliburton's ten-year, no-bid, no-cap contract for Iraq war logistics services, reconstruction, and security is an example. While the government claims that Halliburton is the only company capable of doing the work, the reality is that many companies could do the work. Halliburton's use of subcontractors proves that Halliburton does not possess the capability—or they would not subcontract it—and that other companies do possess the capability—they are actually doing the work—and that Halliburton was awarded the contract through a monopolistic grant for the reconstruction of Iraq. Did the company's former CEO—now Vice President Cheney—exert any influence? This is not free market competition. It is cronyism and betrayal of the public trust.

Halliburton in Iraq is only the extreme case: many outright legislative gifts handed to the pharmaceutical, credit card, military, telecommunications, oil, and mining industries reflect the same policy, the influence of money, and the breakdown of a separation between economics and politics. The right wing feeds its corporate friends and these friends respond with grants to right-wing think tanks, gifts to right-wing churches, and outright financing of political action groups like the 521s and lobbyists. The quid pro quo of these relationships reveals a government-industry relationship similar to that under fascism: the government grants monopolies, contracts, and gifts to corporations, and recipient corporations and their owners keep the government in place. It is neither democracy nor free enterprise, and it is not the legitimate conduct of the people's business.

Totalitarian states are characterized by the convergence of economic and political power into the hands of a powerful few. Totalitarian socialists—as in the Soviet Union and communist

China—exercise state control through planned economies. Totalitarian fascists monopolize and nationalize industry in order to strengthen the state and put it at the service of the state elites. Their primary concern is the control of industry for the purpose of making arms, as in Nazi Germany and fascist Italy. Totalitarian theocrats like the Taliban usurp the drug trade to finance their government and establish the economic power required to control the state. There can be no sustained totalitarianism without such control, official or otherwise. The quid pro quo of corporate-government relationships in America creates a similar confluence of economic with political power, thereby approximating the dynamics of fascism.

HAYEK'S FACTORS FULFILLED

We may concern ourselves with many individual issues, but too often our focus on a particular issue diverts attention from the larger sweep of history. Friedrich Hayek did not miss the big sweeps and neither should we. Individual issues can be argued, debated and rebutted. The resulting diversion of attention is a familiar tactic in our contemporary political discourse. If we stand back from the minutiae, look at where the nation is headed, and weigh what we see against the criteria outlined by Hayek, we gain a real clarity on the national situation. The resurgence of pre-modern consciousness presages a move toward governing structures based on that consciousness. The factors outlined by Hayek and the emergence of pre-modern government are increasingly—and alarmingly—fulfilled. These factors would concern Hayek today:

Factor 1: The articulation of a central organizing philosophy based on the common good and "Ideal Society" is realized by the resurgent Christian fundamentalists with their vision of a moralistic, God-fearing nation. Neoconservatives are supportive of this vision, but less vehement about it.

Factor 2: The distortion of thought and ideas in favor of the Ideal Society vision. Again, the Christian fundamentalists lead this trend with their campaign to re-write history and science, reject the scientific position on evolution while promoting the "intelligent design" theory, and argue that "God's law" is equivalent to the secular law of the United States. Neoconservatives distort facts to bend them to an imperial view of America. Corrupt corporate leaders deny the facts and science of global warming. Right-wing domination of the media, together with skillful use of language and positioning, actively distort and purposely limit the range of political debate.

Factor 3: The loss of real communication between the people. Contemporary political discussions are typified by virulent name-calling, hateful counter-demonstrations, and excoriation of individuals, rather than discussion of issues and reasoned solutions to real problems. Reason loses out to fear in our political discourse; "facts" have become whatever we "believe," a sign that modern liberal principle is giving way to a pre-modern form of consciousness, and real communication is nearly impossible.

Factor 4: The rise of the most ruthless to the top. The political ruthlessness of Tom DeLay, George W. Bush, Karl Rove, Dick Cheney, Bill Frist, and Antonin Scalia is evident in the individual biographies of these men. Although the details differ, they are consistent; they show constant, unbending, personalized belligerence toward all who disagree, and exercise political power through bullying and strong-arm tactics.

Factor 5: The bold, clear, harsh, public handling of dissent. Obvious from the start, the administration's intolerance of dissent is evident in the handling of their own dissenters—Paul O'Neill, Christine Todd Whitman, Richard A. Clarke, Lawrence Wilkerson, and Army Chief of Staff John Shinseki. The IRS has challenged the tax-exempt status of large progressive churches while leaving right-wing churches untouched. Even mild forms of dissent are disallowed—for example, people wearing T-shirts favoring Democratic candidates are routinely denied access to the president's public events. A major example is the impulse to prosecute those who leak the news of secret presidential spying on the American people; the fact of the spying itself is and should be the real outrage.

Factor 6: Citizens become convinced that it is better to trade freedom for security. Such a trade is manifest in the public's willingness to allow Patriot Act invasions and NSA spying on Americans to continue. When we accept these invasions of privacy in the name of security, we in fact trade our freedom for security, thus putting ourselves well on the road toward totalitarian rule.

With the gradual development of the preconditions leading to totalitarianism, many Americans vaguely sense that something is wrong. For others, the ideologies and general movement of the three powerful, right-wing factions are enough. If the ideologies fail to persuade in the light of Hayek's criteria, consider these recent developments during the Bush administration.

THE CONSOLIDATION OF POWER UNDER THE BUSH PRESIDENCY
"I'm the decider."
—George W. Bush

The three primary arms of the right-wing coalition which brought George W. Bush to power bear the ideology necessary to fulfill the conditions which Hayek said leads to totalitarianism. Unfortunately for America, there is in fact ample evidence that the intellectual leanings of this coalition have played out in real, significant ways in American government. While reading Hayek tells us the conditions for totalitarian fascism are increasingly favorable, actual changes in American government under Bush make the prospect of fascism in the next few decades increasingly likely if not yet inevitable.

The *New York Times* revelation of a secret program authorized by the president for spying on Americans, and the resulting firestorm of controversy, should give pause to all Americans of good will to stop and think about what is going on. The issue is not the legality of the NSA program, or even its constitutionality, but limiting the president's exercise of power. The right wing strives to assign to the president virtually unlimited power to set policy and programs in the United States. This theme is becoming increasingly apparent in how this president views his power, a view which presents dire implications for Americans. Here are four pieces of evidence suggesting a move toward dictatorial power.

First, the president established a policy to create a new category of persons, now known commonly as "unlawful combatants," over which *he holds the only authority*. These individuals are designated as unlawful combatants by the president and only the president, and their treatment comes under the jurisdiction of no one but the president and his administration. The legal basis for this designation is the president's own determination, which is not reviewed or approved by anyone else. It functions like a royal decree.

On November 13, 2001, President Bush issued these words in an executive order:

II. Definition and Policy

The term "individual subject to this order" shall mean any individual who is not a United States citizen with respect to whom *I determine* from time to time in writing that:

1. there is reason to believe that such individual, at the relevant times, is or was a member of the organization known as al Qaeda;

2. has engaged in, aided or abetted, or conspired to commit, acts of international terrorism, or acts in preparation therefore; that have caused, threaten to cause, or have as their aim to cause, injury to or adverse effects on the United States, its citizens, national security, foreign policy, or economy, or

3. has knowingly harbored one or more individuals

described in subparagraphs (i) or (II) of subsection 2(a)(1) of this order; and

4. it is in the interest of the United States that such individual be subject to this order.[60]

I have emphasized the two key words in this order: *I determine*. They are important because almost all of the legal justification used to buttress President Bush's authority is based on those two words. In a February 7, 2002, memo, the president further clarified some of his orders:

2d: Based on the facts supplied by the Department of Defense and the recommendation of the Department of Justice, *I determine* that the Taliban detainees are unlawful combatants and, therefore, do not qualify as prisoners of war under Article 4 of Geneva. I note that, because Geneva does not apply to our conflict with al Qaeda, al Qaeda detainees also do not qualify as prisoners of war.[61]

Again the key words are: *I determine*. The emphasis on determination was carefully debated and selected because of the implied ramification described by the Attorney General at the time in a February 1, 2002, memo to the president:

If a determination is made that Afghanistan was a failed State (Option 1 above) and not a party to the treaty, various legal risks of liability, litigation, and criminal prosecution are minimized. This is a result of the Supreme Court's opinion in Clark v. Allen providing that when a president determines that a treaty does not apply, his determination

---

60   *The Torture Papers: The Road to Abu Ghraib*, Memo 2. eds. Karen J. Greenberg and Joshua L Dratel, Cambridge University Press, New York, 2005, p. 26.

61   *Ibid.*, Memo 11, pp. 134–5.

is fully discretionary and will not be reviewed by the federal courts.[62]

In this memo Attorney General Ashcroft shows what the administration was really up to: prevention of federal court review and protection from "liability, litigation, and criminal prosecution." Is it possible they knew what they were going to do, or had already done, to those prisoners? Could they be protecting themselves from the possibility of criminal prosecution? Clearly this entire legal effort and discussion was oriented toward the prevention of "liability, litigation, and criminal prosecution" at least of members of the executive branch and the military.

Second, the president asserted that he alone has the authority to decide who to attack militarily and when to do it. This argument ensured that he had the sole authority to attack Iraq without provocation, and dates to a September 25, 2001, memo from Deputy Assistant Attorney General John Yoo to the president:

> The President may deploy military force preemptively against terrorist organizations or the States that harbor or support them, whether or not they can be linked to the specific terrorist incidents of September 11, 2001.[63]

In other words, the president can invade Iraq on the pretext of links to terrorism, even if the links cannot actually be found. Here is all the legal rationale Bush needed for the Iraq War, fourteen days after 9/11.

Third, the president has argued that our armed forces do not torture, when any American would conclude that the treatment unleashed on prisoners at Abu Ghraib and Guantanamo Bay, the mysterious "alternative methods of interrogation" used in secret CIA prisons around the world, as well as all those actions approved

---

62   *Ibid.*, Memo 9, pp. 126–7.
63   *Ibid.*, Memo 1, p. 3.

by the Secretary of Defense—from water-boarding to mock executions to stress positions—do in fact look like torture. The President
has argued—and tried to maintain—his sole authority to determine
these actions within this administration, and to make them "un-
reviewable" by a court of law or any other legal body. It is here we
find the real reason the Vice President was so opposed to an anti-
torture clause in the 2005 McCain Amendment. When the administration could not win the legislative battle, the president signed
the bill, then immediately signed his own interpretation of the law to
establish a basis for the practices he wants his people to follow. His
interpretation is one paragraph, and here's that paragraph:

> The executive branch shall construe Title X in Division A
> of the Act, relating to detainees, in a manner consistent
> with the constitutional authority of the President to super-
> vise the unitary executive branch and as Commander in
> Chief and *consistent with the constitutional limitations on the judi-
> cial power*, which will assist in achieving the shared objec-
> tive of the Congress and the President, evidenced in Title
> X, of protecting the American people from further terror-
> ist attacks. Further, in light of the principles enunciated by
> the Supreme Court of the United States in 2001 in Alex-
> ander v. Sandoval, and noting that the text and structure
> of Title X do not create a private right of action to enforce
> Title X, the executive branch shall construe Title X not to
> create a private right of action. Finally, given the deci-
> sion of the Congress reflected in subsections 1005(e) and
> 1005(h) that the amendments made to section 2241 of title
> 28, United States Code, shall apply to past, present, and
> future actions, including applications for writs of habeas
> corpus, described in that section, and noting that sec-
> tion 1005 does not confer any constitutional right upon an
> alien detained abroad as an enemy combatant, the execu-
> tive branch shall construe section 1005 *to preclude the Federal
> courts from exercising subject matter jurisdiction* over any existing

or future action, including applications for writs of habeas corpus, described in section 1005.[64] (emphasis added)

Notice the blatant effort to tell the courts to butt out, and the clear indication that adherence to the law remains at the discretion of the executive branch and the Commander in Chief, "... consistent with the constitutional limitations on the judicial power ..." and "... to preclude the Federal courts from exercising subject matter jurisdiction ..." These and other clauses attempt to establish the legal basis for thwarting the law and reserving for the president the choice of whether he follows it or not. The law and the Constitution supply no basis for this declared concentration of executive power.

Fourth, the president has now argued that on authority supposedly granted in the Constitution, and in an act of Congress approving the invasion of Iraq—but which never contemplated spying—he has sole authority to permit the NSA and other intelligence agencies in the U.S. government to secretly spy on Americans without a warrant. In doing this the administration is apparently willing to push the limits of presidential authority so far as to infuriate members of its own party.

* * *

What is consistently alarming about all of these incidents is the assumption of unbridled presidential authority. In each case, the president and his staff endeavored to establish a legal framework to justify the president wielding his power independent of the other two branches of government. Whether that judgment is good or bad, trustworthy or not, protective of the people or not, the fact remains that the president may not act like an old-style king. Before the Enlightenment, kings believed they could do whatever they pleased through "Divine right." When a U.S. President acts this way, the Rule of Law is being displaced by the arbitrary discretion of the

---

64 White House website: President's Signing Statement on HR 2863, emphasis added.

president. Almost without notice, one pillar of liberal democracy is crumbling and we are stepping backward toward a non-democratic, king-centered worldview.

Thoughtful people observe that neoconservative commentators and administration officials openly admit what they are trying to do. Vice President Cheney even made excuses for it to reporters:

> I believe in a strong, robust executive authority, and I think that the world we live in demands it.... I would argue that the actions that we've taken are totally appropriate and consistent with the constitutional authority of the president.[65]

What constitutional authority allows the president to create new categories of people for different legal treatment whom only he can assign to those categories? Such an approach is arbitrary, contrary to the Rule of Law, and no matter what findings the president has signed, violates due process, right to trial, and other protections created explicitly in the Constitution and Bill of Rights to prevent political tyranny.

Consolidation of executive power is also apparent in the claim that a president may authorize an agency of the government to undertake activity that is patently unconstitutional and in violation of the Fourth Amendment guarantees against search and seizure. It is also a flagrant and gross violation of the civil liberties of every American. Wiretapping and collecting data on phone calls without court warrants would be bad enough if it were a mistake. This administration is doing it as a policy and without apology, even though it could easily have gotten the needed warrants via a special court established by the Foreign Intelligence Surveillance Act (FISA). That court was set up to create a constitutional mechanism for obtaining warrants when such searches are time-sensitive. President Bush decided unilaterally that the FISA court was insuffi-

---

65   *Boston Globe*, as quoted on http://www.truthout.org.

cient and began monitoring phone calls without any documentation of legitimate justification. Only the president's people decide what to listen to, know who is listened to, and act on the listening. No check, no balance. The executive branch takes total discretion, thus creating legal structures supporting arbitrary law, which is a most dangerous attack on the basic principle of the Rule of Law.

New policies regarding the treatment of prisoners further illustrate the consolidation of executive power. Despite the long-established national and international agreements for the proper treatment of prisoners, President Bush has claimed the right to re-interpret these as he sees fit. The President determines Afghanistan is a failed state, that the Geneva Convention does not apply, that U.S. Courts may not intervene if he keeps prisoners in Guantanamo, that U.S. law can be overridden by using presidential findings and determinations, that he alone can approve kidnappings, secret renditions, secret CIA prisons in Eastern Europe, and horrendous treatment of prisoners at the hands of the U.S. Military and CIA. Although the end result of all these acts and policies is reprehensible, the crime against the Constitution and liberal democracy lies in the claim of executive power to unilaterally establish such policies.

Perhaps most troubling of all, the courts and Congress have frequently allowed these actions to pass; when faced with likely defeat, the administration has sought ways to get the decision out of the hands of courts and Congress. By preventing adverse court decisions and re-interpreting laws, the administration maintains the power it claims for itself. In other cases, it wins the acquiescence of the other branches, thereby enabling the executive branch to claim legitimacy even as it wields power that increasingly resembles dictatorship. We must remember that while an act may be technically "legal," that does not mean it conforms to Rule of Law. Most dictatorships are, in fact, "legal."

CRONYISM: STATUS OF THE GOVERNMENT AND THE CURRENT REALITY

If anyone doubted the dangerous arrogance of this government before the 2004 election, certainly events since the election have removed all doubt. Many writers and publications have expressed concern about the deceit and outright lies of this administration on matters of critical national importance. The progressive press, including magazines and newspapers like *Democracy Now!* and *Mother Jones*, has uncovered the lies, catalogued them, and debunked them. Traditional conservative commentators like Bob Barr and columnists in *American Conservative* have done the same. Yet the lies go on, and the right wing wins an election and stays in power. Many have expressed concern over the right wing's profound arrogance of power displayed in cronyism. Since the election, several events have occurred which validate these concerns. Some of the most significant are:

- Bush has replaced all resigning cabinet secretaries with people he knows well and controls from within the White House. Anywhere else in the world this is known as cronyism. It indicates a dangerous narrowing of the already thin band of thinking which controls the national government. That narrow thinking included the assumption everything would go well in Iraq at no cost to the taxpayers. America would be greeted as liberators. $275 billion, 2,700 dead Americans, and 18,000 seriously wounded Americans later, we are not seen as liberators, but as occupiers who are likely there for less altruistic reasons.

- The new CIA chief, Porter Goss, hastened the exodus of career CIA professionals, all replaced with political appointees, mostly former staff from his days at the House of Representatives. The CIA was supposed to be a-political, just gathering the facts and giving them to policy-makers. Although politicization of the agency first became overt with the appointment of George H. W. Bush as head of the CIA in 1975,[66] there is increasing evidence of enormous political distortion of the intelligence used to justify the invasion of Iraq.[67] The appointment of Goss and his housecleaning activity took politicization further than ever

---

66   Trento, Joseph J. *Prelude to Terror*. Carroll & Graf, New York, 2005.

67   Bamford, James. *A Pretext for War*. Doubleday, New York, 2004.

before. Goss resigned in May 2006, and was replaced by General Michael Hayden, the man who operated the NSA's secret programs spying on Americans over the previous five years (2001–2006). Once again we have "insider" people with similar views in leadership positions, and no room for dissent among the thinkers, strategists, and planners at the agency. This would be dangerous at any time in history but never more than now; the American people, propagandized into being afraid, are willing to give up their rights for perceived increased security, and put far too much trust in their government.

- Normally the Attorney General could be expected to help mitigate potential abuses by agencies like the CIA, but the new Attorney General, Alberto Gonzalez, has—as White House Counsel—already shaped the policy which has condoned torture at Guantanamo Bay, torture at Abu Ghraib and across Iraq, the holding of prisoners without cause, NSA spying on Americans without warrants, and total presidential power to make war that is "un-reviewable" by any other branch of the government. As the architect of the legal argument for concentrated executive power, the new Attorney General spent President Bush's first term justifying abuses and concentration of power. Gonzalez is now the chief law enforcement officer in the nation, the man charged with protecting the American people, their freedoms and rights and bringing offenders to justice. Gonzalez, like Goss and Hayden, comes from Bush's inner circle.

- The Republican Right has threatened to use the so-called "nuclear option" with respect to Bush's judicial appointments. The purpose of this effort is to rebuild the federal judiciary with people who hide their opposition to the freedoms of liberalism under terms such as "constructionist" and "original intent."[68]

---

68 "Original intent," for example, is a code phrase which would undo virtually every civil rights legislation ever passed as unconstitutional because the framers of the constitution did not "originally intend" to include women, blacks, Jews, or any other minority in their protections.

Although the press discusses the issue as if the Republicans want to simply change the rules, this measure is much more draconian. The "nuclear option" involves using Vice President Cheney to overrule the Senate Parliamentarian in an unprecedented move to thwart the 200-year-old right to filibuster. This maneuver demonstrates the outrageous lengths to which the Bush administration and its right-wing allies will go to get their way, and their disregard for deliberative balance and broad consensus in selecting judges. Their vision is of a more "Christian, neoconservative, power elite-friendly" set of judges sitting on the federal bench and Supreme Court in lifetime appointments.

It is not alarmist to mention that fascism means leadership by the elite. Right-wing elites rule the executive branch and lead the legislative branch. Two new Supreme Court justices have associations with the elite right wing as well. These leaders come from all three right-wing sectors: some are "Christian" like Tom DeLay; some are neoconservative like Dick Cheney and Donald Rumsfeld; some are corporate like John Snow. Only George W. Bush combines the three—an apparently avowed Christian, power hungry and committed to empire, whose utter failure in business uniquely "qualifies" him to gut the national government without damaging his reputation. The names may change but the right-wing elites maintain their positions of power. Whether through intention or not, their continued rule leads us ever closer to the conditions under which fascism flourishes.

Although we can find plenty of transgressions committed by our government, our elected officials still derive their power from the people and in many ways reflect who we are. The external threat documented in the video footage when the World Trade Center came crashing down signaled an inner challenge: Are we up to the long-term demands of liberty? Or are we ready to surrender the gift of liberty so many fought and died for over the centuries? Are we equal to the rigors of modern consciousness? Or will we regress into the dark recesses of pre-modern thinking? Only we—not the government, not the legislature, not the courts—we the people stand able to defend our own liberty. How we respond will be a test of our American character.

REBUILD TRUST: CREATING SECURITY IN A FREE COUNTRY

Security policy in a free nation must be built on the bedrock of the people's trust in their government and law enforcement. No nation can be free and secure without such trust and we cannot defeat al Qaeda without it. The real choice we face as a nation is not between security and freedom—as if we must exchange one for the other— the choice is between a free nation—where increased freedom means increased security—and a police state—where reduced freedom means reduced security. This distinction must be central to any discussion of national policies aimed at keeping the country secure.

A free and secure people have high levels of trust in their police and military to properly carry out the responsibilities assigned to them. People must be able to trust the police to use their powers wisely and in the interest of the people, not to turn their guns and powers on the people unnecessarily or arbitrarily. They must trust the military not to torture or mistreat those held in detention, and they must trust the police not to engage in corruption. Rogue individuals may break the codes of conduct, but trust prevails that the *institution* is focused on honorable behavior and will deal appropriately with perpetrators within its ranks. In the wake of Abu Ghraib and Guantanamo problems, NSA spying, and constant lies and deceit from leaders, many Americans have ceased to trust institutional leadership.

Such trust is essential to security in a liberal society because securing a free nation requires the participation of the people. Tips and information from the public, along with investigations by police lead to apprehension of perpetrators and prevention of attacks and crimes. The many arrests resulting from the TV show *America's Most Wanted* testify to this reality. So do the potential attacks by al Qaeda that have been prevented since the early 1990s, and the investigations that show our government had the information necessary to prevent the attacks on September 11, 2001, but could not piece it together properly. At the end of runways of major airports, huge temporary signs now flash: "Report Suspicious Activity" and give a phone number. As corny as it sounds, the signs reflect a reality: the police depend on the participation of the people to help them secure a free society.

As trust in authorities erodes, increasing numbers of citizens become reticent to "report suspicious activity." Why? Because decent people do not unnecessarily subject their fellow citizens to abuse at the hands of anyone, even their own police. Trust is eroded when we suspect that those reported will not be treated properly, that arbitrary arrest, improper search, mistreatment, and even torture may result. Decent people will not unnecessarily subject others to such treatment. People may report to authorities if they are *certain* behavior is suspicious, but usually their information is incomplete. Being uncertain, most citizens do not report to authorities who are untrustworthy. As a result there will be an erosion of liberty, law, and order and the ability to enforce the law and protect the citizenry, all of which are proper concerns of progressives, moderates, and conservatives alike.

The re-establishment of trust in military and police authority is crucial to defending the nation. With Donald Rumsfeld as head of the Defense Department and Alberto Gonzalez running the Justice Department and the FBI, the restoration of trust remains remote. Congressional investigation, oversight, and checks and balances are necessary. The press should dig into these issues and inform the people. Resignations can be demanded, but President Bush has made it clear he intends no such change, so the only remedy will be at the polls. If we are fortunate, a more enlightened, thoughtful leadership will shore up the trust which is the source of our security.

THINGS TO REMEMBER

- In 1944, Friedrich A. Hayek, a darling of the modern American right-wing movement, identified six cultural conditions necessary for a country to fall into fascism: The Ideal Society, distortion of truth, corruption of words, rise of the ruthless, intolerance of dissent, and the people's willingness to trade freedom for security. Those conditions are present today in America, and their source is the right wing.

- The right wing consists of three groups: neoconservatives, the Christian Right, and corrupt right-wing corporate elites.

- Those in the Republican Party and administration who dissent suffer ruthless character assassination by a comprehensive media machine—not just the administration, but also the media mouthpieces of the right-wing movement.

- The Bush administration continues to claim unprecedented powers for the president and has built a legal structure to justify them. Always watch for the word "lawful," which means they are claiming something that most Americans don't think they have the right to claim.

- The concentration of power in the presidency is a harbinger of totalitarian rule, if the country continues to move in this direction.

CHAPTER 5

Al Qaeda's Challenge

AL QAEDA—AN ISLAMIC FUNDAMENTALIST GROUP PRACTIC-
ing *Jihad*—attacked America on September 11, 2001. Most Americans still do not understand al Qaeda because our leaders have
failed to help us understand. Our ignorance enables those leaders
to describe al Qaeda in ways which are politically beneficial to them.
We were led to believe that al Qaeda, the Taliban, Saddam Hussein,
the Iraqi insurgents, and the Palestinian groups Hamas and Fatah
are all essentially the same. They are all mere "haters of freedom," as
Bush said. "You are with us or you are against us." This perception
is a convenient lie for the American leadership—one that enabled
it to make many Americans think invading Iraq was part of a retaliation for the 9/11 attacks or a strategy for dealing with terrorism.
The truth is that Iraq had nothing to do with al Qaeda or 9/11, and
the Palestinian groups refused to participate in 9/11. Although fundamentalism is a significant branch of Islam—as it is in Christianity—conflating the large variety of peoples, perspectives, and
persuasions which make up Islam and treating it as a monolithic
culture is a mistake—and one which we make at our own peril.

More importantly, our continued ignorance of al Qaeda has led
the American people to absurd acts. When al Qaeda attacked us,
we knew where they were located, made a partial attempt to defeat
them, and then invaded a country thousands of miles away that had
nothing to do with their attack or their organization. Whatever the
Bush administration's real motives may be, our collective ignorance

acquiesced in the decision. As a result, al Qaeda is not defeated despite the enormous expenditure of our national resources.

As an American, I too, was ignorant of al Qaeda on September 11, 2001. Certainly, I was aware of the name bin Laden and the problems and conflicts of the Middle East. But over the five years since 9/11, I sought to understand al Qaeda itself—where it came from, the origins and sources of its power, and the intensity of its hatred that would create an event like 9/11. In this chapter, I present four main discoveries which have implications for policy, and which may serve as a basis for further study by American citizens.

- First, the common Western misperception of Islam as a unified, monolithic movement may not be accurate. Islamic religion, culture, and ethnic diversity create an endless diversity of ideas, concerns, and issues among Muslims. Only one set of those attitudes is Islamic fundamentalism.

- Second, Islamic fundamentalism arises out of forces similar to those which created Christian fundamentalism nearly five hundred years ago: the confrontation between traditional, premodern religion and liberal modernity.

- Third, al Qaeda and Osama bin Laden are driven by strategic objectives which make the Palestinian-Israeli issue strategically tangential, but quite convenient politically.

- Fourth, these insights will help us debunk common American misperceptions.

THE DIVERSITY OF ISLAM

For far too long, Americans have viewed Islam through a narrow-focus lens. Perhaps the mistake can be overlooked while distorted images from 9/11, Madrid, and London are burned into our minds along with phrases like "haters of freedom," which was used so often by the president. Whatever its source—demagoguery, fear, or ignorance—we cannot allow ourselves to perpetuate this.

Olivier Roy, Professor at EHESS—The School of Advanced Studies in Social Sciences in Paris—provides a more realistic view of contemporary Islam. Islam is the dominant religion in many countries—from Malaysia to Morocco—and a significant minority religion in many others, including European countries, Russia, and America. Islam as a religion is constantly infused with the cultures in which it is practiced. As Roy points out:

> ... why does one systematically confuse Islam and Arab culture under the absurd concept of 'Arabo-Muslim' societies? Arab societies include Arabic-speaking Christians and Jews, while most of the world's Muslims are not Arabs.[69]

Is there Islamic influence on Arab culture? Yes. Is there Arab influence on Islam? Yes. But the notion that identifies the two with each other is misguided. Roy comments on our American confusion:

> The culturalism approach is reinforced by the confusion between Middle East and Islam. In particular the Israeli-Palestinian conflict tends to shape in the United States the debate on Islam. There is a constant confusion between Muslims and Arabs. Most of the examples used to show that Islam has a problem with modernity deal with the Arab Middle East, but not with Malaysia or Turkey.[70]

Perhaps nowhere is this view of Islam more detrimental to American policy than in the perception that the Israeli-Palestinian crisis is the source of the terrorism problem. Roy is clear on this:

> One cannot understand the current process of Islamic radicalization by focusing almost exclusively on the Middle East crisis and the Arab world. Of course, both the Israeli-Palestinian conflict and the invasion of Iraq have led to a crys-

---

69   Roy, Olivier. *Globalized Islam.* Columbia University Press, New York., 2004, p. 12.

70   *Loc. cit.*

tallization of anti-U.S. and anti-Western feeling among a section of Muslim youth. But this connection remains symbolic. The new generations of radicalized Western Muslims do not go to Palestine to fight the infidels: they went to Afghanistan, Chechnya, Bosnia, Kashmir and, of late, Iraq; they go to New York, Paris and London. The time and space of modern Islamic radicalism is emancipated from the Middle East. It is a global space.[71]

While a sophisticated understanding of Islamic religion, Muslim culture, and the process of globalization are all necessary in order to understand Islamic radicalization, *Jihad*, and al Qaeda, we apparently make a mistake when we confuse al Qaeda with the Israeli-Palestinian problem. Is there a relationship? Yes, but not one of union or cause. To predicate thinking, analysis, or policy on the illusion that solving the Israeli-Palestinian problem will solve terrorism is more likely to lead to tragic, mistaken decisions like invading Iraq, which was based on a similar conflation.

Most Americans understand that Christian fundamentalist leaders like James Dobson and Pat Robertson do not speak for all Christians. Nor are issues that concern these men deeply—such as gay marriage—necessarily of concern to mainline Christians or non-religious Americans. Neither does Osama bin Laden speak for Islam or all Arabs. No doubt Islamic fundamentalist leaders and Christian fundamentalist leaders have similar political and structural goals, even though the substance of the goals—the specifics of what they want in their society—is different. As Roy said:[72]

> Common to all fundamentalist or reformist movements is a quest to define a "pure" religion beyond time and space.

Let us, then, take a look at the Islamic fundamentalist theology on which al Qaeda and bin Laden base their appeal.

---

71   *Op. cit.*, p. 13.
72   *Op. cit.*, p. 11.

AL QAEDA'S RELIGIOUS ROOTS

Sayyid Qutb,[73] an Egyptian, is generally regarded as the most influential thinker and writer contributing to the ideological and theological underpinnings of present day *Jihad*. In the 1950s he became the leading thinker of the Muslim Brotherhood—a radical, fundamentalist Islam organization originating in Egypt in 1928—edited its journal and defined its direction. Qutb apparently found himself in a deep internal struggle to maintain his extreme views. Paul Berman writes:[74]

> Yet all the while [Qutb] had to struggle, as he confesses in his pamphlet *Milestones*, against his own liberal impulses—'the cultural influences which had penetrated my mind in spite of my Islamic attitudes and inclination.'[75]

Fundamentalism of all kinds finds itself in collision with liberal principles. As with the Christian version, Islamic fundamentalism is built on pre-modern consciousness, whereas liberal principle derives from modern consciousness that differentiates sacred from secular and places authority squarely with the individual.

In his analysis, Qutb sees a great "hideous schizophrenia" in Christendom brought about by its own principles.[76] The split derives from the common schisms of Western culture: reason versus inspiration, science versus dogma, and liberalism versus fundamentalism. These rifts arise within liberal consciousness as it evolves away from the honor-order-duty consciousness of the Middle Ages. Qutb says Islam must confront the same schizophrenia. In Islam the split creates a conflict of monstrous and frightful proportions, because Qutb's Islam insists there can be no separation of church and state, no division between God and society.

---

73 Pronounced $\overline{koot}'$-āb.

74 Berman, Paul. *Terror and Liberalism*. W. W. Norton & Company, New York-London, 2003.

75 *Op. cit.*, p. 62.

76 *Op. cit.*, pp. 68–76.

On the contrary, American liberalism insists on the separation of church and state, which makes it completely untenable to Qutb's brand of Islam. For Qutb, Islam cannot be fully practiced in a state that does not implement Islamic law (*shariah*). The separation of life into different aspects—the modern differentiation of church, state, and self characteristic of liberalism—impedes the fulfillment of an Islamic life. The crisis in Islam's fundamentalism arises because the advancement and diffusion of this schizophrenia via the media and Muslim migration has desecrated and damaged Qutb's fundamentalist Islam.[77]

Pre-modern religious consciousness that refuses to develop becomes fundamentalism when it confronts modern consciousness, and it often espouses violence. Christianity confronted modern consciousness during the Reformation when Calvin's sixteenth century fundamentalist theology instigated the French Religious Wars. The violent history of Christianity's confrontation with modernity in the sixteenth and seventeenth centuries led Olivier Roy to suggest that Islam is going through a similar confrontation today:[78] a traditional religion founded on pre-modern consciousness and rituals confronts a powerful, liberal modern consciousness. As society tries to grapple with the changes, violence and war are the result. The difference is that modern technology greatly expands the implications, reach, and potential deadliness of the violence.

The religious confrontation is intended to defend Qutb's fundamentalist Islam against the onslaught of Christian-based liberal-

---

77   If Qutb sees the confrontation ideologically/theologically, and he sees the major threat not as military or economic, but as an infection of the mind with liberal values, the response of the Islamic world to the war in Iraq can be understood clearly. Bush declared that he is going to try to spread liberal democratic values in the Arab world, according to Qutb exactly and precisely that which threatens Islam the most. In essence Bush has declared holy war on them. It is his ignorance here—or worse, his purposeful offense against Muslims—which creates the legacy with which America will be dealing for decades.

78   Roy, *loc. cit.*

ism and other non-Islamic values outside the Islamic world.[79] Qutb accuses not only liberalism, but the Zionists, the Christian crusaders, and even communism. He also identifies an enemy within: those who call themselves Muslims but champion non-Islamic ideas. He reserves his harshest criticism and the harshest punishment for them. His treatment of "false Muslims" mirrors the treatment reserved for "false Christians"—who are not "born again" by fundamentalist standards—and "false Republicans"—moderate Republicans who cannot countenance the right-wing radicalism of the present party power structure. Qutb argues for the idea of a "pure vanguard"—a term we see in bin Laden's rhetoric—the pure Muslims ready to save Islam through whatever means necessary, acting on the harshest ethics of an eye for an eye, and a tooth for a tooth.

In typical paternalistic, totalitarian fashion, Qutb spins an ideal, utopian vision of Islamic society. Assuming all members of the society are Muslims practicing devoutly by the standards of *shariah*, he envisions universal freedom, universal right, and universal justice. As God's law, *shariah* is the supreme expression of human freedom because it ensures that no man is subjugated to another man, but only to God. But Qutb's vision of freedom admits exceptions similar to those one finds in Christian fundamentalism. Berman quotes Qutb:

> Islam has guaranteed to women a complete equality with men ...; it has permitted no discrimination except in some incidental matters connected with physical capacity, with customary procedure, or with responsibility, in all of which the human status of the two sexes is not in question.[80]

Are not these "incidental matters connected with physical capacity, with customary procedure, or with responsibility" the very

---

79   Berman, *op. cit.*, p. 92.
80   *Ibid.*, p. 96.

basis of inequality, used to "keep women in their place" in nine-teenth century America? Are they not similar to the oft-quoted biblical command to wives to "submit to your husbands"? These phrases rationalize gender bias throughout the world. Qutb is not offering freedom, but only the illusion of freedom cloaked in religious rhetoric.

Qutb is specific about improving society. He declares the "just" penalties for the unspecific crime of threatening the "general security of society." Again, Berman quotes Qutb:

'As for those who threaten the general security of society, their punishment is to be put to death, to be crucified, to have their hands and feet cut off, or to be banished from the country.' And, having reviewed those several punishments, Qutb brightly concluded, 'On these foundations, then—an absolute freedom of conscience, a complete equality of all mankind, and a firm mutual responsibility in society—social justice is built up and human justice in ensured.'[81]

This is where Qutb's theology begins to deviate from most contemporary Christian fundamentalism. Qutb explicitly calls for violence, laying the theological foundation for totalitarian *shariah* that came to pass in Taliban-controlled Afghanistan in the mid 1990s, along with despotic kidnappings, rapes, and public executions. In addition to calling for the return to traditional *shariah*, Qutb also establishes the theological basis of *Jihad*: justification for martyrdom and violence—including suicide bombing—in order to defend the faith and achieve paradise. Here, he exhorts the soldiers of Allah:

The *Surah* tells the Muslims that, in the fight to uphold God's universal Truth, lives will have to be sacrificed. Those who risk their lives and go out to fight, and who are prepared

---

81   *Ibid.*, p. 97.

to lay down their lives for the cause of God are honorable people, pure of heart and blessed of soul. But the great surprise is that those among them who are killed in the struggle must not be considered or described as dead. They continue to live, as God himself clearly states.

To all intents and purposes, those people may very well appear lifeless, but life and death are not judged by superficial physical means alone. Life is chiefly characterized by activity, growth, and persistence, while death is a state of total loss of function, of complete inertia and lifelessness. But the death of those who are killed for the cause of God gives more impetus to the cause, which continues to thrive on their blood. Their influence on those they leave behind also grows and spreads. Thus after their death they remain an active force in shaping the life of their community and giving it direction. It is in this sense that such people, having sacrificed their lives for the sake of God, retain their active existence in everyday life....

There is no real sense of loss in their death, since they continue to live.[82]

Qutb's Islamic utopia is a total vision in which Islam defines the totality of the individual, the society and the state. Theologically, he established the idea of complete devotion through the image of the martyr who lives on through his blood. *Shariah* clearly defines the political structures, with justice meted out by the *mullahs*. Islamic law further defines the economic structures, including outlawing interest payments on debt. This vision is holistic: Islamic self, Islamic society, Islamic state, with Islam informing all three spheres of religion, economics, and politics. Islam is to infuse everything, or it is not real Islam. From Qutb's viewpoint real Islam can only be real if it enwraps the totality of the human being—i.e., it must be totalitarian.

---

82   *Ibid.*, pp. 101–102.

Western liberalism implicitly judges this vision of Islamic utopia as abhorrent, just as it does the Christian fundamentalist vision. Qutb's view is anti-historical in seeking to eliminate hundreds of years of improved social understanding and push Islam back fourteen hundred years. It is anti-liberty in that it allows no freedom of conscience or thought, but substitutes an absurd version of freedom which demands ideological consistency. In fact, Qutb's vision of Islam is directly opposed to every major principle of liberalism.

After Qutb died, his form of fundamentalist Islam was propagated primarily by the Saudi-funded *Wahabbi* schools. The Saudis built over fifteen hundred schools and mosques around the world, focused children on literal readings of the Koran—as Qutb counseled—and indoctrinated the children with fundamentalist theory. This created a climate in which an inspirational leader was needed to sustain the movement, and Osama bin Laden became that leader.

AL QAEDA'S LEADERSHIP AND PURPOSE

When fundamentalism informs education, it generates a fundamentalist worldview—economic, religious, and political ideologies—that goes with it. The result is an economically disaffected, emotionally resentful, spiritually hardened cohort confronting daily images of modernity in the media and society. In the 1980s, with no one articulating that hatred and directing it toward America, most of the Muslim world directed these frustrations toward the Arab regimes in power. Bin Laden took up the huge task of redirecting that anger toward America, which he saw as the leader of a Western attack on Islam. His success relies on the ideological base of fundamentalist Islam created by Qutb in the middle of the twentieth century and propagated by Saudi oil money. Bin Laden's rhetoric now shapes the worldview of millions of Muslims worldwide.

If Qutb was the great theologian of fundamentalist, militaristic Islam, then Osama bin Laden is its great inspiration and organizational genius. The line from Qutb to bin Laden is almost direct, passing through Abdallah Azzam.[83] Azzam was not a leading thinker or theologian like Qutb was, but a fiery orator and inspirational fundamentalist Muslim theologian influenced heavily by Qutb. Azzam—a university professor when bin Laden was in school—was in Pakistan when bin Laden went there to initiate his part in the *Jihad* against the Soviets. Azzam was killed in a car bomb explosion in 1989, but he remains an influence on bin Laden's theological direction.

Osama bin Laden developed a network through his schooling, business operations, and time in foreign countries, especially in Sudan where he personally worked with Hassan al-Turabi, leader of the National Islamic Front in Sudan—the real power broker behind the regime from 1989 to 2001. Bin Laden's years fighting the Soviets in Afghanistan were also pivotal to his networking and radicalization. In terms of his role in the threat to America, he emerges onto the world stage with the formation of al Qaeda in about 1990, and the deep offense he took when "American infidels" were allowed onto Saudi soil in the first Iraq War and bin Laden's own offer to defend the kingdom was spurned. With al Qaeda, bin Laden began his outspoken leadership on the issues of Islam and the incitement of *Jihad* against America.

Bin Laden came to the formation of al Qaeda and leadership of *Jihadism* with a unique set of credentials:

- A distinguished war record fighting for Islam against the Soviets in Afghanistan in the 1980s.

- A personal fortune estimated at $300 million.

- A fundamentalist piety that is honored by many in the Muslim world.

- A spartan lifestyle that provides credibility to the commitment of his cause.

- A financial and organizational savvy that enables him to put his ideas into operation.

83　Burke, Jason. *Al Qaeda: Casting a Shadow of Terror*. I. B. Tauris, London, 2003, p. 68.

- A set of messages which say put Allah first, Islam is great, defeat the crusaders, and stop injustice. These inspire many Muslims, especially those who are fundamentalist in their views.

In short, bin Laden is a unique person with unique attributes on which Al Qaeda was built. In the few months after 9/11, bin Laden's death, arrest, or capture would probably have dealt a major blow to al Qaeda, and generally to the *Jihadist* movement. When America failed to accomplish that single goal, al Qaeda developed contingency plans, decentralized the organization, and created a new strategy for global, decentralized *Jihad* based on the work of Mustafa Setmariam Nasar. Under the pen name Abu Musab al-Suri, Nasar published a sixteen-hundred-page treatise titled *The Call for a Global Islamic Resistance*. Craig Whitlock, writing for the *Washington Post*, describes the book this way:[84]

[It] outlines a strategy for a truly global conflict on as many fronts as possible and in the form of resistance by small cells or individuals, rather than traditional guerilla warfare. To avoid penetration and defeat by security services, he says, organizational links should be kept to an absolute minimum.

In late 2004, three years after 9/11, Nasar outlined the decentralization strategy and published it on the Internet, indicating Al Qaeda was moving beyond bin Laden.

Bin Laden rose to prominence with a simple strategy: successful execution and delivery of a strong message of inspiration and hope to his Muslim followers. In carrying out attacks he found a way to garner the publicity he needed to get out his message. From the formation of al Qaeda around 1990 to September 11, 2001, al Qaeda has successfully executed the following attacks:

---

84 Craig Whitlock, "The Architect of the New War on the West," in *The Washington Post*, May 23, 2006. http://www.msnbc.msn.com/id/12914965.

- February 1993—Bombing the World Trade Center, New York
- October 1993—Killing U.S. soldiers, Somalia
- June 1996— Bombing Khobar Towers, Saudi Arabia
- August 1998—Bombing U.S. embassies in Kenya and Tanzania
- October 2000—Bombing the USS Cole, Yemen
- September 2001—Destruction of the World Trade Center and attack on the Pentagon
- April 2002—Bombing of a synagogue, Tunisia
- May and June 2002—Bombings against American targets, Pakistan
- October 2002—Night club bombings, Bali
- May 2003—Bombings in Riyadh, Saudi Arabia, and Casablanca, Morocco
- August 2003—Bombing a hotel, Jakarta, Indonesia
- November 2003—Bombing a housing complex in Riyadh, Saudi Arabia
- November 2003—Bombing synagogues in Istanbul, Turkey, and a follow-up bombing of a British bank in Istanbul
- March 2004—Bombings in Madrid
- May 2004—Hostage-taking in a Saudi oil company
- July 2005—Three bomb attacks on the London underground and one on a London bus.

Each attack has helped bin Laden promulgate his message. Most Americans don't think bin Laden even has a message because our leaders keep demonizing him. If we are to deal effectively with this enemy we need to more clearly understand him and what he wants.

WHY DOES BIN LADEN HATE US?

There is one essential reason bin Laden detests the West: he believes that the West has been attacking Islam both physically and with our liberal ideas since the fall of the Caliphate nearly one hundred years ago. This position derives its ideological power from Qutb, its popular power from the *Wahabbi* schools and its deadly violence from bin Laden's skill as an organizer, public figure, and terrorist. Bin Laden believes Islam and the Islamic people have been constantly under siege. Here is a bin Laden excerpt:

> We say that the brutal enemy does not need documents or excuses for continuing that war he has started against Islam and Muslims many decades ago. For God's sake, what are the documents that incriminate the Palestinian people that warrant the massacres against them, which have been going on for more than five decades at the hands of the Crusaders and the Jews. What is the evidence against the people of Iraq to warrant their blockade and being killed in a way that is unprecedented in history. What documents incriminated the Muslims of Bosnia-Herzegovina and warranted the Western-Crusaders, with the United States at their head, to unleash their Serb ally to annihilate and displace the Muslim people in the region under UN cover. What is the crime of the Kashmiri people and what documents do the worshippers of cows possess to make them sanction their blood for more than fifty years. What have Muslims in Chechnya, Afghanistan, and the Central Asia republics committed to warrant being invaded by the brutal Soviet military regime and after it communism's killing, annihilating, and displacing tens of millions of them. What evidence did the United States have the day it destroyed Afghanistan and killed and displaced the Muslims there. It even launched prior to that the unfair blockade of Afghanistan under UN cover. Under the same cover Indonesia was ripped apart; Muslims were forced to leave Timor.... Under the UN cover too, it intervened in Somalia, Killing and desecrating the land of Islam there. It is even the first to urge the Crusade ruler in the Philippines to annihilate our Muslim brothers there. There are many other count-

less issues. We say that all the Muslims that the international Crusader–Zionist machine is annihilating have not committed any crime other than to say God is our Allah.[85]

Although the events he cites are real, bin Laden's perspective is warped by his doctrinal religious and cultural views. For example, he pays no attention to the past history of Islamic *Jihad*, terrorism, and religious arrogance that created deep resentment against Islam in many parts of the world. Yet, this quotation gives a hint of bin Laden's fury. He sees himself as defending his sacred and beloved religion and all its people. Bin Laden claims he wants the Muslim people left alone to practice Islam their way, with integrity and wholeness. Muslims understand this and many carry a similar view of the transgressions of the West. They know of these events, and they nod their heads, "Yes, they are attacking us!" Many Muslims agree with bin Laden when he complains about the immorality of the West. They see us on their television screens or in their cities, and can come to no other possible conclusion. It is bin Laden's mission—his duty as he sees it—to inspire these Muslims to *Jihad*. While he appeals to a sense of justice for Islam, he also presents a utopian vision consistent with Qutb. Conveniently left out of his rhetoric are the details of Taliban rule in Afghanistan: disappearing young women, systematic rape, stadium executions, forced dress codes and religious practice, all hallmarks of totalitarianism. The rhetoric supporting totalitarian regimes always glows with idealism and utopian visions. Just as Auschwitz and the Killing Fields were the grim realities of Hitler's and Pol Pot's utopias, Taliban Afghanistan is the real-world incarnation of bin Laden's utopian vision.

INCITING THE FAITHFUL

Al Qaeda is transformed—in the words of al-Zawahiri, bin Lad-

---

85   Scheuer, Michael. *Imperial Hubris: Why the West Is Losing the War on Terror.* Brassey's Inc., Washington, DC, 2004, p. 130.

en's first lieutenant—into "the vanguard of a Muslim nation that decided to fight you to the last breath and not surrender to your crimes and vices."[86] The echo from Qutb is unmistakable. But bin Laden's incitement message goes further, and is deeply religious in its intention and tone:

> I must say that my duty is just to awaken Muslims, to tell them as to what is good for them and what is not.... Al Qaeda was set up to wage *jihad* against infidelity, particularly to counter the onslaught of the infidel countries against the Islamic states. *Jihad* is the sixth undeclared element of Islam. Every anti-Islamic element is afraid of it, al Qaeda wants to keep this element alive and active and make it part of the daily lives of Muslims. It wants to give it the status of worship.[87]

War as worship, *Jihad* as defending religion, suicide as martyrdom. According to bin Laden, all are required of "true" Muslims. Bin Laden's appeal to Muslim youth works the same way and he is clever and appealing to the masses. The "martyrs" achieve the highest, most holy places, according to bin Laden's fundamentalist faith and Qutb's doctrine, and the young believe it. The cleverness rests in the honoring of suicide attackers. Bin Laden may be sincere, but that makes him no less seductive. The evidence is in his words honoring the nineteen hijackers of 9/11:

> The brothers, who conducted the operation, all they knew was that they have a martyrdom operation and that we asked each of them to go to America but they didn't know anything about the operation not even one letter. But they were trained and we did not reveal the operation to them until

---

86   Statement on Al-Jazeera TV, Sept. 10, 2003, as quoted at http://jamestown .org/terrorism/news/article.php?articleid=2369530.

87   Scheuer, *op. cit.*, p. 131.

they are there [in the United States] and just before they boarded the planes.

Michael Scheuer, the former director of the CIA's program to track bin Laden, which the Bush administration has since disbanded, comments:

> What the West heard in bin Laden's voice as cynicism and cruel manipulation, was heard by Muslims for what it was, a quietly and proudly spoken elegy by a man overcome by awe and admiration for the unquestioning young men who willingly defended Islam with their lives.[88]

Bin Laden's fundamentalist rhetoric has continued in subsequent statements:

> The men understood that *jihad* for the sake of God is the way to establish right and defeat falsehood. They understood that *jihad* for the sake of God is the way to deter the tyranny of the infidels.... These men sought to prepare a response for the Day of Reckoning. Faith in God and the Hereafter and emulating the traditions of Mohammed, may God's peace be upon him, is what prompted them to leave their homes....[89]

Inspiring words. They ask for the ultimate commitment, the ultimate demonstration of allegiance, the ultimate act of honor: carrying out one's duty to God. The word defines a standard for those—especially the young—who are fully committed to their God. Fundamentalist Islam is a religion of extreme commitment, providing fertile ground for the acceptance of these ideas. Bin Laden makes sense to fundamentalist Muslims; he inspires them.

---

88   *Op. cit.*, p. 136.
89   *Loc. cit.*

ORGANIZATION

The evidence for al Qaeda's organization comes from the news: Al Qaeda training manuals found in bombed houses or abandoned cars near terrorist operations, a computer which includes all the casing images of American buildings found by Pakistani intelligence, training camps spread throughout Afghanistan before the American invasion displaced the Taliban, and tunnels and hiding places built throughout the Afghanistan–Pakistan border area. Attacks like the ones in London in early July 2005, are coordinated. Websites get the word out, and video tapes go out as in a standard PR campaign. Al Qaeda protects itself by providing information only on a need-to-know basis. For example, Al Qaeda sent twenty men to the U.S. to carry out an attack, yet the men apparently did not even know what the mission was until it was launched.

Organization and discipline falter as operations move away from the center. Cells are broken up, and individuals lose discipline. People like Zacharias Moussawi often blow their cover, get arrested on unrelated issues, and expose plots wherever competent police work occurs. Al Qaeda may be far flung, but its macabre successes are a testament to bin Laden and his organizing ability. He spawned al Zarqawi in Iraq, and cells and operations around the world.

Bin Laden remains central to al Qaeda. He has built, organized, and inspired a network to carry out *Jihad* against America. He focuses the network and expands its vision and reach. He inspires his lieutenants and leaders, as well as much of the Muslim world. Bin Laden is the man to take down, but the benefits of doing so have diminished with al Qaeda's re-organization in the wake of the American invasions. Because of the Bush administration's failure to stop bin Laden early, and al Qaeda's ongoing effort to decentralize, al Qaeda will remain a threat to our liberal principles and nation for a long time to come.

AL QAEDA'S STRATEGY AND TACTICS

Al Qaeda's strategy has worked on selected goals over the years. First, it consolidated Muslim anger from the disparate resentment of local regimes to a focus on a far off, amorphous, yet visually clear enemy: the West, and especially America. Bin Laden has consistently targeted the U.S., thereby turning the focus of the entire Muslim world on the U.S. When Muslims get angry today it is more likely to be against the U.S. and the West than against their own totalitarian regimes.

Second, al Qaeda seeks to re-establish the Caliph as the head of the Muslim world, much as the pope is head of world Catholics. Qutb wrote that one Muslim nation would have to come to the forefront; here the Caliphate could be re-established and assume world leadership for all of Islam. When Afghanistan repelled the Soviet invasion, bin Laden targeted Afghanistan as that leading nation and a few years later the Taliban rose to power under his guidance.

America's failure to secure the peace after invading Iraq created a strategic opportunity for al Qaeda, of which they are taking full advantage. Al Qaeda in Iraq got started *after* the war began, and enraged Islamic *Jihadists* continue to flow into the country for the opportunity to fight the United States. The strategy is to destabilize the nascent government there, in hope that destabilization will prepare the road for control of the government by al Qaeda.

The post-9/11 world brought about changes in bin Laden's inspirational messages to his followers. Bin Laden's messages were amplified when the United States attacked Iraq, in that his pronouncements seemed prophetic to Muslims worldwide. He claimed the West was attacking Islam in a war of civilizations. He claimed America is an imperial nation. In a complete blunder of foreign policy rhetoric, the Bush administration further incited bin Laden's followers by declaring a "crusade"—a term with historically deep and offensive meaning to Muslims—whose stated goal is to bring "democracy"—which many Muslims hear as "liberal decadence"—to the Middle East. These unwise words were repeated across the Muslim world, reinforcing bin Laden's claim that this was an attack on Islam, Bush's claims to the contrary notwithstanding.[90]

---

90   Burke, *op. cit.* This is the theme of Burke's book—al Qaeda as a decentralized, loosely knit movement, and becoming even more so after 9/11.

The tragedy of the Bush administration's response to 9/11 is that it strengthened al Qaeda by not defeating it decisively. While many Americans feel that "the world changed after 9/11," al Qaeda also changed. While maintaining its focus on its goals, al Qaeda adjusted its strategy in three significant ways after 9/11:

- **Decentralize Leadership:** Decentralization is the effort to make al Qaeda unbreakable by creating leaders in many places. Although the organization already was decentralized, bin Laden remained the core leader. Today, al Qaeda can act more independently without bin Laden's direct involvement, and is far more likely to survive if he is eliminated. For example, the Madrid and London attacks were carried out by affiliated but independent al Qaeda groups: "home grown" terrorists.

- **Broaden the Attacks on Western Democracies:** The new strategy has a widened focus that includes America, but also other Western countries and their apostate friends in the Muslim world. Separate the people of Western and apostate regimes from their governments through the use of fear and indiscriminate killing that the governments cannot stop. Do it in a way that appeals to the religious sensibilities of fundamentalist Muslims in order to win their approval, support, and new recruits.

- **Obtain, Justify, and Use Nuclear Weapons:** While trying to obtain nuclear weapons, build the rhetorical case for their use against America.[91] Osama bin Laden is preparing the world, and especially his Muslim admirers, for an attack on the United States which will produce mass casualties. He has been consistent in this message since 9/11.

Ultimately, Islamic terrorists aim to create totalitarian theocratic states based on *shariah*. If we are to defeat theocratic totalitarianism, we must prevent the al Qaeda movement and others like it from taking control of a nation. Nations can muster resources

---

91 Scheuer, *op. cit.*, pp. 152–160.

which movements cannot, and they have status in the world. Governments will play *real politick* with nations in a way that they will not with movements.[92] The Bush administration has used fear of nuclear annihilation to scare the American people and as a justification for its invasion of Iraq and ongoing confrontation with Iran. But the stance it has taken has infuriated people across the world, making precisely such an attack infinitely more likely than it was the day of 9/11.

Today, we must not be afraid; we must be *determined*. Al Qaeda is not some deep dark, unknown, unforeseen group erupting suddenly from the shadows. They are not the random pathological killer shooting for the joy of the kill. Rather, al Qaeda has an ideology, a financial structure, a charismatic leader, a strategy, and a tactical plan. Al Qaeda can be understood and with a more thorough understanding, free nations can first protect themselves, and second vanquish the enemy. Most importantly, we can avoid the wasteful commitment of time, energy, and resources spent in fighting the wrong enemy at the wrong time in the wrong place. If we lose ourselves in fear or blind ourselves with the stupidity of our current leadership, we risk all that America is and was ever meant to be.

American liberalism will stand up and fight for itself. In World War II we sacrificed as a nation in order to achieve a common objective. We stood up during the Civil War when liberal principles—including the rights of minorities—were at stake. And we will do so again against al Qaeda. But we cannot win based on fighting

---

92 Pakistan, for example, sold nuclear secrets to what we would call "bad" governments around the world. But as far as we know, Pakistan has not sold such secrets to political groups. There is a reason for this: governments have a sense of self-preservation which political groups generally lack. Governments have something to lose. Desperate freedom movements will stop at nothing for they have nothing to lose. Governments can tax people, are internationally recognized, and control vast resources. An al Qaeda–like theocratic fascism governing a nation would be very, very dangerous indeed. It could stimulate similar movements in other countries, and turn last century's "red tide" into a new sweep of Islamic fundamentalist theocracies across the Islamic world.

non-terrorists. The travesty of our current situation is that we have not engaged and did not vanquish the enemy. Our retaliation was incomplete, we attacked a different nation, spread our resources too thinly, and bolstered the enemy through stupid policy and profound ignorance on the part of our political leadership. Liberalism will never submit, but neither will it win in a blind rage. It will study the weakness of the enemy, and strike at that weakness to fully defeat him. Years after 9/11, our right-wing government leadership has utterly failed to accomplish this goal.

CONFRONTING AL QAEDA

Critics of the Bush administration's War on Terror have been attacked as weak on terrorism. Administration supporters claim the critics have no plan, allow themselves to be blackmailed by terrorists, and do not understand the real nature of the threat. Yet, the administration has no actual plan for fighting terrorists—even though they have war plans for Iraq and Iran—and allow themselves to fall into a reactionary response, execute that response incompetently, and profoundly misunderstand the terrorist threat. The results of their approach speak for themselves: Osama bin Laden remains at large five years after 9/11, al Qaeda is growing, and our military is exhausted in a country where terrorists had been no threat previously, but now attack daily. Somalia is being ruled by al Qaeda-style Islamic fundamentalists. Whether because the Bush administration committed a grand folly, or purposely confounded terrorism policy with a foreign policy goal of "benevolent hegemony"—a neoconservative policy term that essentially means "friendly imperialism"—the results speak for themselves. Their policy has failed to establish democracy, and failed to defeat the terrorists.

America can do better. It is abundantly clear to any informed observer that while terrorism is real, the "War on Terror" is contrived. We cannot make our anti-terror policy contingent on solving every problem in the Middle East. Because we accept the War on Terror as a reality and predicate anti-terror policy on Mid East politics, we have failed to focus on our real enemy: al Qaeda. The goal is specific: defeat al Qaeda. The enemy is clear: it is al Qaeda. We should not engage in a so-called War on Terror; we should focus on and defeat al Qaeda.

REFOCUS ON AL QAEDA

Therefore, it seems to me that America can refocus its policy on al Qaeda. The American people will likely rally around a strategic direction that focuses on the real enemy, clarifies American interests, executes a plan for defending them, and uses a proportionate response to defend the nation.

As part of that, we may need to stop fighting the insurgency in Iraq, which is a fundamentally Iraqi problem, an embryonic civil war. America does not belong in the middle of it, and it is unlikely that we can win a civil war against an insurgency in a foreign country. Military history demonstrates that no matter how strong one's army is, a visiting force cannot win against rebellions which are supported by the local population. Senator Joseph Biden and former Senator Gary Hart have each proposed alternatives to President Bush's "stay the course" directive. These and other plans are viable; it is time to choose one and move beyond the president's foolish stubbornness.

But moving on does not mean leaving the country. Iraqis will need to work out their government and their security situation. But America has unfinished business with al Qaeda. Like it or not, al Qaeda is now in Iraq. We should eliminate security patrols, policing operations and other such activities in Iraq and hand those functions to Iraqis; our armed forces should remain for only one reason: to search out and destroy al Qaeda. When the mission to destroy al Qaeda is either completed or deemed impossible, then we leave Iraq.

A military strategy built on these lines seems far more reasoned and rational than "staying the course" in Iraq and picking a new fight with Iran. The staying the course strategy fails to confront al Qaeda, which is our only legitimate security concern. Instead, we have stepped into their game and played our part exactly as they would have wanted it. But if we simply pull out, given what has happened, we leave an enormous problem behind us and we do not achieve our objective of defeating or arresting al Qaeda and its leadership. We have the skill and ability to focus resources on the real enemy; we are missing only the competent and thoughtful leadership required to take us there.

THINGS TO REMEMBER

- Al Qaeda has its own vision, goals, and strategy. It is not synonymous with the Israeli–Palestinian conflict, even though that conflict is sometimes used in the litany of bin Laden's complaints against the West and has a deep appeal to Muslim populations.

- Islamic fundamentalism is similar in ideology and style of consciousness to Christian fundamentalism; both detest liberalism and the separation of church and state. However, the *Jihadists* of Islamic fundamentalism are far more violent than their Christian fundamentalist counterparts.

- Qutb is the Islamic fundamentalist theologian who created the ideological basis for al Qaeda in the 1960s.

- Bin Laden has articulated al Qaeda's key goals: purify Muslim lands of the infidels; take over a nation and re-establish the Caliphate; obtain, justify, and use nuclear weapons.

- We must better understand this enemy or we shall make additional, colossal blunders like the invasion of Iraq.

- It may be time for a new strategy. America has played al Qaeda's game, much to our own detriment. We may not be able to leave the mess we have created completely, but we can at least focus on the real enemy. Only that will create the security we crave.

CHAPTER 6

Individual Liberty and the Corporate Entity

THE ROLE OF CORPORATIONS IN LIBERAL SOCIETY IS BOTH HOTLY debated and ideologically contrived. The far left never met a corporation that was acceptable to them, and the far right cannot see corruption when it hits them in the face. For the last few decades, the radical right-wing ideology of free market dogma has dominated the debate. No matter which side is dominant, corporate structure, not corporate actions, is the underlying issue. As such, the erosion of liberty at the hands of corporate structures is the most dangerous and insidious of the three contemporary challenges to liberalism.

The corporation is one of America's strongest tools in building the power and creativity of our economy. But the very features of corporate organization that make it such a powerful creative economic engine—aggregation of capital, freedom from investor liability, the lack of corporeal mortality, and the privilege of exclusive economic focus—are precisely the features which have grown to threaten the ongoing development of liberal democracy. The non-regulation of corporate entities under free market dogma will destroy American liberty just as effectively and inevitably as state ownership. A corporate-owned state would be just as bad as the state owning corporations.

My argument is against these two extremes. Corporations are vital to economic creativity and so should not be controlled by the state. In the same way, the vital political creativity of the citizen's voice should not be overpowered by corporate economic power deployed in the political sphere. Balance must be maintained. The democratic-liberal state and the corporations in the economy should thrive in a balance properly worked out through regulation, incentives to behavior, and political rhetoric. The worst outcome for liberal democracy occurs when corporations build enormous economic power and use it to drive public policy. When that occurs, state and corporate interests turn against the people, their democracy, and their freedom. We know the name for that: it is fascism.

A PRIMER ON THE MODERN CORPORATE STRUCTURE

A corporation is a simple legal structure established to allow people to pool capital for economic ventures in such a way that the sole risk for the "owners" or "investors" is the potential loss of their investment. It is also a legal framework for organizing the conduct of business. Three characteristics distinguish the corporation from any other form of organization: freedom from personal liability of the investors, the ability to amass large amounts of capital, and an unlimited lifespan—corporations never expire. The result is that corporations win a privilege granted by government to focus exclusively on the development of profit and the creation of wealth. These features are closely related, and are the reason some of the founding fathers, such as Jefferson and Madison, viewed corporate entities with mistrust.

The exclusive focus on financial outcomes is a privilege that was bestowed in early America only when some public good was intended as an outcome associated with a corporation. Over time, incorporation has become almost an economic right of all business people, so much so that incorporating, which in early America required an act of the state legislature, is now a mere administrative action involving a nominal fee and the completion of a form. This legal structure underlies America's great economic expansion, creativity, and prosperity over the past 120 years. Many of the freedoms we enjoy are possible only because corporations enable private citizens to pool capital for their own purposes without a state or a church to inter-fere. We owe much of our American prosperity to the legal struc-tures and traditions which developed because of privileges granted to the corporate entity. But as corporate power reaches beyond the economic sphere and threatens to dominate our political culture, the power of the people to self-govern erodes along with the neces-sary separation of economics and politics.

FREEDOM FROM PERSONAL LIABILITY

The freedom from liability provision of corporate organization is a sweeping power that shields the business owner-investor from risking his or her personal assets: home, car, investments, personal belongings. Any debt or lawsuit brought against the corporation may damage the corporation's ability to continue in business, but will not cost the owner-investor his own assets. While the owner-investor or CEO can be prosecuted for criminal acts—such as murder, theft, or fraud—he or she cannot be held personally responsible in civil court for merely "irresponsible" acts of the corporation.[93]

When a business has only one or a few owners, this provision amounts to protection against liability lawsuits. The litigiousness of today's society makes incorporation essential to almost any busi-ness because the most minor mishap or disagreement can provoke a lawsuit. The unincorporated business person puts his or her own home, car, and other assets at risk in addition to the business.

The legal freedom from personal liability also separates own-ership from management responsibility. Without this provision an individual shareholder—as an owner of the company—could be held liable for any debts the corporation may incur, whether result-ing from lawsuit or general business practices. Without this protec-

---

93   There are exceptions to this, as when officers or directors of a corporation, for example, violate their fiduciary responsibility to shareholders, they may be sued by those shareholders. Also, there is always the possibility of frivolous shareholders lawsuits against officers and directors. As a result, many pur-chase Directors and Officers insurance to protect their own assets.

tion, for example, if Wal-Mart borrowed ten million dollars from a bank for working capital, a Wal-Mart stockholder could be held responsible for a share of the ten-million-dollar debt if the company defaulted on the loan. The corporate structure insulates the investor from this responsibility.

While legal language uses the word "liability," the more common phrase is "freedom from *personal responsibility*." In other words, investor-owners may reap profits from an entity with no responsibility for actions taken to gain those profits. Herein lies both the creative power and the tyranny of the corporate structure: the freedom from personal responsibility enables *and forces* the corporate manager to focus on a single responsibility: corporate profit. The American corporate structure unleashes tremendous economic creativity, the result of which is American wealth, economic power, and standard of living. Simultaneously, the corporate structure imposes a kind of economic tyranny that separates the interests of business from the more human interests of the owners, operators, and employees. Tension develops at the individual, organizational, and societal level that is inherent to all corporations, whether they behave poorly or responsibly.

This intrinsic tension in the corporate structure cannot be reliably and consistently mediated by "social responsibility" or "business ethics," except insofar as it affects profitability. Even with an enlightened, thoughtful leader, lack of sufficient cash flow and capital remain the only potential threat to the corporation's existence. Such leaders are forced to focus on and convert business activity into bottom-line results. Corporate structures have no inherent interest in the benefit to communities of people—nations, states, regions, or towns—or communities of nature—forests, wetlands, threatened species—precisely because the corporate structures were created to avoid those concerns. When we look at poisons being emitted by a smokestack, unfair labor practices, outsourced jobs, the destruction of community and nature, or other externalities,[94] we ask,

---

94 "Externalities" is an economic term referring to real costs created by an activity that are not born by the generator of that activity. Pollution is the most common example, but there are others as well.

"Who can be held responsible for this?" The response is an eerie and awful answer: No one can be held responsible for this.

The modern corporate structure is designed to relieve managers from all responsibility save one: profit for the shareholders. That single responsibility guides and directs all decisions, and when it does not guide those decisions, the corporation fails. The classic example is Bill Norris, CEO at Control Data Corporation in the 1970s. Norris idealistically intended to make Control Data Corporation a major player in building communities and making the world a better place. He used corporate funds for a range of projects from incubating small businesses to community development projects. In his enthusiasm for these projects Norris lost sight of the constraints within which he worked as a corporate officer. After years of his visionary—yet neglectful—leadership the company lost millions of dollars, laid off hundreds of workers, and Norris was forced to resign. The company never recovered and was eventually bought out.

The point is that while Norris had a genuine interest in the good of the community, he failed the corporation which, by design, requires focus on *its* goals, and allows focus on the community only insofar as is consistent with the corporate mission. "Social responsibility" in corporate life can only be sustained as a method of public relations for the purpose of maintaining a good image in the community. Good corporate citizenship—while preferable to bad citizenship—fails to alter the basic requirements of corporate behavior.

Another excellent example of the corporate responsibility ethic involved the Union Carbide disaster in Bhopal, India. Jerry Mander describes it this way:

> In 1986, Union Carbide Corporation's chemical plant in Bhopal India, accidentally released methyl isocynate into the air, injuring some 200,000 people and killing more than 2,000. Soon after the accident the chairman of the board of Union Carbide, Warren M. Anderson, was so upset at what happened that he informed the media that

he would spend the rest of his life attempting to correct the problems his company had caused and to make amends. Only one year later, however, Mr. Anderson was quoted in Business Week as saying that he had 'overreacted,' and was now prepared to lead the company in its legal fight against paying damages and reparations. What happened?[95]

Mr. Anderson first reacted to the disaster as any human being would; then his role as head of Union Carbide required him to act according to a different set of principles. As head of the corporation he recognized no other responsibility but the company's profitability. It might be possible to criticize Mr. Anderson for his moral failing as a human being, but that is beside the point; had he stayed with his original reaction, he certainly would have been replaced as the head of the corporation by someone more amenable to the corporate goal.

Leaders like Bill Norris and Warren Anderson, like most CEOs and mid-level managers, are good people locked into a set of values which they are powerless to change. The corporate structure demands that human concerns give way to corporate concerns. Human concerns can play a role only so long as the corporate goals are achieved. Free markets and individual integrity have been tried, and they do not work. The problem is deeper than that.

CAPITAL

The second unique characteristic of the modern corporation is the ability to amass huge quantities of capital. Capital can be amassed largely because of the guarantee of freedom from personal liability; otherwise, all owners would have to take a personal interest in the day-to-day activities of the corporation. General Electric Corporation would become unworkable with its millions of sharehold-

---

95   Mander, Jerry. *In the Absence of the Sacred*. Sierra Club Books, San Francisco, 1992, p. 126.

ers. But without liability, capital can come from many different sources—hundreds or thousands or millions of investors—and capital can be aggregated at a level that would be impossible otherwise.

Today, corporations operate on a whole new order of magnitude. Some corporations, for instance, have more capital at their disposal than many nations. In my home town, free enterprise became a sham when a local corporation bought all the homes in an entire neighborhood, razed them, and built strip malls and parking lots where people once lived. This was not replacement of blighted homes or redevelopment for the community; all were perfectly good, functioning homes with two-car garages, three bedrooms, and other desirable features, including an occasional swimming pool. It was a result of concentrated wealth and power. Zoning laws were changed to serve powerful interests, and the neighborhood lost out. The homes were replaced with parking lots and a community was destroyed.

None of this is new, it is only new to America. American corporations with their huge accumulations of wealth have behaved similarly in developing countries for over a century. Companies like Dole and United Fruit virtually defined the concept of "banana republic"—Third World countries controlled by corporations for the production of fruit for America. The corporation's ability to control land, backed by the power of their capital, has destroyed the communities which once thrived on the lands the corporations control, and impoverished the residents.[96] This domination would not have been possible without the corporate legal structure that enables a few people to amass and control the required capital.

The aggregation of capital enables the expansion of "scale." There is not a single environmental problem that cannot be linked to the problem of "scale," and every one of them is a direct result of it. Acid rain results from huge, coal-fired power plants, which could not be built without enormous amounts of capital. A quart of paint thinner spilled in a backyard creates a local problem, but an indus-

---

96   See Lappe, Frances Moore. *Food First*. San Francisco, 1977.

trial site with hundreds or thousands of barrels of paint thinner waste is an environmental disaster waiting to happen. Coal cannot be mined from strip mines without huge equipment requiring enormous capital. Ozone depletion in the atmosphere is inextricably linked to gargantuan quantities of chlorofluorocarbons released into the air. Carbon dioxide build-up is occurring from what Paul Hawken calls the "once-in-a-million-years hydro-carbon blowout sale," which requires thousand-mile pipelines, huge drilling rigs, and giant refineries, spewing all kinds of chemical compounds into the air.[97] The abandonment of rural communities is directly connected to the development of chemical pesticides and huge machinery for farming conglomerates. All these problems of scale require aggregated capital, and each results in the loss of individual freedom among those citizens affected by the activity, yet not profiting from it.

The ability to amass capital in today's economy is more far-reaching than ever before. Decisions regarding the use of capital tend to emanate from the top down, much as in a centrally-planned economy. Those decisions often seem utterly disconnected to the reality of a particular factory, community, or individual. Although no democratic or community control is exercised or invited, these decisions often affect a public resource: air, water, land, people. Under the auspices of free trade, capital can be moved around the world faster and more easily than ever before, making corporate entities truly global, while local attempts at controlling their behavior are thwarted by the same free-trade treaties. Most major new capital investments—even at corporations—require the approval of the Board of Directors. With corporations beginning to dwarf entire nations in terms of economic size, these boards look more like global politburos dividing the economic landscape into fiefdoms than they do institutions of freedom and democracy. The impact on individual freedom and the liberal values that built this nation is profound.

---

97   Hawken, *op. cit.*

NO SUNSET: CORPORATIONS NEVER DIE

The third unique feature of corporations is that they never die from natural causes. Corporations may be bought out, go into bankruptcy, or be dissolved by the board, but they are rarely forced to liquidate. On the other hand, human beings always liquidate assets at the end of their lives. Inheritances are broken up and spread out to the heirs, estate taxes are paid, and philanthropy is often chosen as a final gift offered by the deceased. Lacking mortality, corporations disperse their assets only through sale, bankruptcy, or dissolution. Otherwise, the aggregation of capital goes on endlessly.

As a result, corporate planning has only one goal: continue to expand the business and its effective use of capital. There is never an end to its pursuit of return on investment, which means it keeps growing and controlling more and more resources. Continued growth satisfies investors, but enormous domination of a market can lead to unsatisfactory externalities. Corporations never reach a point of "satisfaction," but they grow indefinitely; they must, or betray the trust placed in them by the investors.

The real implications of this thinking are evident in the recent strategic plans of the largest corporations. For example, under former CEO Robert Goizueta, Coca-Cola began to measure its market penetration in terms of the total percentage of human fluid intake globally. Goizueta had said that at 2 percent of total human fluid intake, Coke had plenty of room to grow. Likewise, Wal-Mart is reported to measure its goals in terms of total u.s. GDP. At $258 billion in sales, the company accounts for 2 percent of u.s. GDP, and is the nineteenth largest economy in the world. Critics have revealed that Wal-Mart long term growth objectives are to account for 25 percent of total u.s. GDP. That is the scale on which corporate entities are thinking.

Corporations that accumulate too much economic power tend to use it to gain political power and advantage. Often, the result is the use of political leverage to hide, cover, deny, or address hidden structural economic problems with the corporation's business. For example, American corporations (General Motors, Firestone Tires, and Standard Oil) used their accumulated economic power to eliminate public transit in many cities in the 1930s and 1940s in an effort to grow the market demand for cars.[98] They formed a company, National City Lines, which bought over one hundred public transit lines in fifty cities for the specific purpose of shutting them down. Today, oil companies influence energy legislation to focus on oil and marginalize alternatives. High oil prices serve their interests, so they seek relentlessly to protect and leverage their investments in order to increase their return; this is totally consistent with the corporate structure and charter. Credit card companies and their lobbyists write a bankruptcy bill that serves their interest in collection, at the expense of the notion of forgiveness that is inherent in the old bankruptcy protocol. The influence to achieve these results derives from the concentration of wealth in corporate hands, and it is exercised in the political sphere in alignment with the logic of corporations. If allowed to undertake such actions, corporations must undertake them. It is part of their fiduciary responsibility to shareholders to do so; but it is also to the detriment of liberal democracy.

HISTORY OF THE CORPORATE STRUCTURE IN AMERICA
To gain historical perspective it is instructive to look back through the history of the development of the corporate entity in America. The early Americans who defeated the British and wrote the Constitution fought not only against the King of England, but more significantly against the rights granted by the King to the corporations which were exploiting the colonies. Chief among these were the monopolies granted by Parliament in 1773 to the East India Company, a corporation chartered in 1600 by Queen Elizabeth I. The company had long enjoyed a monopoly for the importation of tea to England, but with the Townsend Acts and the ensuing American boycott, the company had fallen on hard times; it had a glut of tea on

---

98   Snell, Bradford C. *Statement of Bradford C. Snell before the United States Senate Subcommittee on Antitrust and Monopoly*: Presented at hearings on the ground transportation in connection with S1167, February 26, 1974.

its hands and nowhere to sell it. The stockholders, ship owners, and other powerful figures in England were so closely connected to the fortunes of the East India Company that Parliament had to act, so they granted the company a monopoly on tea trade with the American colonies. Tea was the quintessential American drink at the time, much as coffee is today, so these laws affected nearly everyone in the colonies. The first three shipments of East India Tea had been turned away by those to whom it was addressed in New York, Philadelphia, and Charleston. The governor of Massachusetts was to receive the tea in Boston. He refused to allow the tea to be sent back and threatened to destroy the ships if they tried to leave Boston Harbor. The Sons of Liberty—a local group of patriots led by Samuel Adams and John Hancock—dumped the tea into the harbor rather than allow it to be brought ashore. The "Boston Tea Party" was thus a protest not simply against the tea tax, but against the corporate power of the East India Company.

Early American history abounds in debates over the powers granted to corporations. The power to charter a corporation was vested in the state legislatures on the principle that the citizens could control the corporation through democracy. Early American corporations had to operate under very strict rules and legislatures chartered them for specific periods of time and controlled their profit levels and activities. The rationale for these controls was that the corporation must act for the public good in order to enjoy the privileges of incorporation. According to the Supreme Court of Virginia in 1809, if a corporation's "object is merely private or selfish; if it is detrimental to, or not promotive of, the public good, they have no adequate claim upon the legislature for the privileges."[99]

Over a long period of judicial rulings, however, most of the powers of legislatures to control corporations waned. The onset of the diminishment of legislative authority started in an 1819 case. The Supreme Court determined that the U.S. Constitution prohibited New Hampshire from revoking a corporate charter granted to

---

[99] Currie's Admin. v. Mutual Assurance Society, 4 H&M 315 (Va. 1809).

Dartmouth College by King George III in 1769.[100] Massachusetts legislator David Henshaw remarked, "Sure I am that, if the American people acquiesce in the principles laid down in this case, the Supreme Court will have effected what the whole power of the British Empire, after eight years of bloody conflict, failed to achieve against our fathers."

Legislators responded to the 1819 ruling by writing clauses of revocation into the articles of incorporation which they granted, reserving unto themselves the right to make these determinations. But the slow erosion of democratic sovereignty and community control over corporate power had already begun. The history of the growth and development of the corporate power follows a line of Supreme Court decisions which gradually increased the *political* rights of corporations. One list of these decisions, with a summary of their impact, is instructive:[101]

- Trustees of Dartmouth College v. Woodward (1819)
  Corporate charters are ruled to have constitutional protection.

- Munn v. State of Illinois (1876)
  Property cannot be used to unduly expropriate wealth from a community (later reversed).

- Santa Clara County v. Southern Pacific Railroad (1886)
  The substance of this case (a tax dispute) is of little significance, but this fateful case subsequently was cited as precedent for granting corporations constitutional rights.

- Noble v. Union River Logging Railroad Company (1893)
  A corporation first successfully claims Bill of Rights protection (5th Amendment)

- Lochner v. New York (1905)
  States cannot interfere with "private contracts" between workers and corporation—marks the ascension of "substantive due process."

---

100 *Dartmouth College v. Woodward*, 17 U.S. 518 (1819).

101 http://www.reclaimdemocracy.org/personhood/#significant.

- Liggett v. Lee (1933)
  Chain store taxes prohibited as violation of corporations' "due process" rights.

- Ross v. Bernhard (1970)
  7th Amendment right (jury trial) granted to corporations.

- U.S. v. Martin Linen Supply (1976)
  A corporation successfully claims 5th Amendment protection against double jeopardy.

- Marshall v. Barlow (1978)
  The Court creates 4th Amendment protection for corporations—federal inspectors must obtain a search warrant for a safety inspection on corporate property.

- First National Bank of Boston v. Bellotti (1978)
  Struck down a Massachusetts law that banned corporate spending to influence state ballot initiatives, even spending by corporate political action committees. Spending money to influence politics is now a corporate "right." Justice Rehnquist's dissent is a recommended read.

- Central Hudson Gas v. Public Service Comm. of NY (1980)
  This oft-cited decision concerns a state ban on ads promoting electricity consumption.

- Austin v. Michigan Chamber of Commerce (1990)
  Upheld limits on corporate spending in elections.

- Thompson v. Western States Medical Center (2002)

- Nike v Kasky (2002)
  Nike claims California cannot require factual accuracy of the corporation in its PR campaigns. California's Supreme Court disagreed. The U.S. Supreme Court took up the case on appeal, then issued a non-ruling in 2003.

As noted above, the seminal case was the 1886 decision in *Santa Clara County v. Southern Pacific Railroad*.[102] This case was later cited

---

102   118 U.S. 394 (1886).

as the one in which the Supreme Court ruled that a private corporation was a natural person under the U.S. Constitution, and is thus sheltered by the Bill of Rights and the Fourteenth Amendment. It was a monumental decision that enabled courts to strike down most legislative controls on corporations and became the basis of judicial reasoning in striking down several laws meant to protect citizens from corporate harm, including labor laws, legislative control of corporate entities, and the use of corporate money for political purposes. But shockingly, the issue was never argued before the court. David Korten, author of *The Post-Corporate World, Life After Communism* described it this way:[103]

> Far more remarkable, however, is that the doctrine of corporate personhood, which subsequently became a cornerstone of corporate law, was introduced into this 1886 decision without argument. According to the official case record, Supreme Court Justice Morrison Remick Waite simply pronounced before the beginning of argument in the case of *Santa Clara County v. Southern Pacific Railroad Company* that
>
> "The court does not wish to hear argument on the question whether the provision in the Fourteenth Amendment to the Constitution, which forbids a State to deny to any person within its jurisdiction the equal protection of the laws, applies to these corporations. We are all of opinion that it does."

The court reporter duly entered into the summary record of the Court's findings that:

> "The defendant Corporations are persons within the intent of the clause in section 1 of the Fourteen Amendment to the

---

103 Korten, David. *The Post-Corporate World, Life After Capitalism.* San Francisco, Berrett-Koehler, 1999.

Constitution of the United States, which forbids a State to
deny to any person within its jurisdiction the equal protec‑
tion of the laws."

Thus it was that a two‑sentence assertion by a single
judge elevated corporations to the status of persons under
the law, prepared the way for the rise of global corporate
rule, and thereby changed the course of history.

Although the decision was roundly criticized by many sub‑
sequent jurists, including Chief Justice William O. Douglas, the
precedent had been set. Perversely, the rights instituted in the
Constitution and Bill of Rights to protect citizens from autoc‑
racy, authoritarianism, aristocracy, and totalitarianism were used
to liberate the very power from which such rights were supposed
to protect the people.[104] The 1886 decision became the basis for
declaring labor unions conspiracies and pitting police and mili‑
tia against striking workers who were already being exploited and
abused. Nonetheless the ruling prevailed, the infrastructure was in
place, and by the early 1900s, slightly more than two dozen cor‑
porate trusts controlled over eighty percent of production in their
markets. A congressional committee stated in 1941 that "The prin‑
cipal instrument of the concentration of economic power and wealth
has been the corporate charter with unlimited power...." That char‑
ter may have been transformed by activist courts over the course of
time, yet it remains the legal basis of corporate existence today.

UNDERSTANDING THE THREAT

Many critics lament the concentration of wealth in corporate cof‑
fers. Economic freedom can get swept up in this concentration.
When a multitude of small, independent businesses—bookstores,
main street stores, and small farmers are examples—are undercut

---

104 Addressing the decision sixty years later, Justice William O. Douglas wrote,
"There was no history, logic or reason given to support that view."

in their communities by huge corporate enterprises like Wal-Mart, Barnes & Noble, and Archer Daniels Midland—we see the effects of concentration. On a purely economic basis, there is good reason to be deeply concerned.

The spillage of this enormous *economic* power into *political* power—the ability of the corporation to have deleterious effects on society through political action rather than economic action—is far more dangerous and insidious. When corporate entities take political action, they do so within the ethical goals of the corporation, i.e., to increase their ability to improve shareholder returns. However, many activities that result in improvements in returns do not serve the public, workers, consumers, or any interested parties other than shareholders—and the shareholder interest is conceived only narrowly, in terms of return on invested capital. When corporations are better able to promote their political agenda because of economic advantages given them purportedly in the public interest, politics and liberal democracy become warped. Economic power translates into political power, thus breeching the critical yet seldom discussed separation of business and state.

INSTITUTIONS OF CORPORATE POWER

While the legal and political rights of corporations have grown and developed through the courts, the people running the corporations rapidly became our nation's elite leaders—and later, the global corporate elite. As elites, these people had many common interests, and they created formal and informal methods of communicating with one another about those interests. Probably because they are elite public figures, but also private individuals with much at stake, such working together regularly brings about claims of conspiracy. Sometimes, small groups of this elite do conspire or engage in corruption. But at the same time, people with common interests have always come together to discuss and defend those interests—it is human nature. What is unique is the enormous economic power such people wield, and how they use it to gain the political control they need to further strengthen their interests.

Since WWII, these common interests grew into a series of institutions which reflect the emergence of the global elite. They arose in three stages. First, the Bretton Woods Conference (1944) gave rise to the International Monetary Fund (IMF) and the World Bank. This was significant because in order to charter these organizations, the signatory countries had to agree to subject currency values to international disciplines. All currencies were pegged to the U.S. dollar to determine value. In essence, this resulted in the first major loss of sovereignty to countries who no longer controlled currency values. It was the precedent on which future agreements would draw in order to further erode national sovereignty, and in the case of democracies, true democratic control.

Even today, the Bretton Woods Committee continues this work, and shows the close connection of the first conference to the organizations that followed. Here is the Bretton Woods Committee mission statement:[105]

> The Bretton Woods Committee is a bipartisan group of distinguished citizens dedicated to increasing understanding of the vital role the international financial institutions play in promoting growth and stability for the U.S. and global economy. We believe that the United States must work to maintain its leadership position and cooperate closely with other governments through the "Bretton Woods Institutions"—the World Bank, the regional development banks, the International Monetary Fund and the World Trade Organization.

The statement clarifies the purpose of these international institutions: preserve the leadership and prosperity of the United States as understood by "distinguished citizens." Such a purpose may be useful and important, but we should not deceive ourselves or be misled into thinking such organizations do anything else. Leader-

---

105 http://www.brettonwoods.org/.

ship and prosperity are understood through the corporate-shaded lenses, and the international bodies such as the World Bank serve those interests primarily.

Second, in the 1970s, the Trilateral Commission, the World Economic Forum (WEF), and General Agreement on Tariffs and Trade (GATT) emerged from essentially the same impetus as Bretton Woods. These organizations updated the treatment of the global economic order, which was necessary because Europe and Japan were both emerging from post-WWII reconstruction as economic powerhouses. From the standpoint of American corporate and political elites, Europe and Japan needed to be brought into the economic fold. The Trilateral Commission was specifically targeted to this goal.

As with Bretton Woods, the ordinary people were left out. Labor, workers, the middle class, the poor, the hungry, and the environmentalists all go unrepresented. The mechanism for exclusion is mostly money: The World Economic Forum, for example, requires a $70,000 annual fee for an individual participant, and $250,000 for a corporate membership. And because money is so critical to the political process, politicians pony up in order to gain the access they need, just as the corporate elite do to get access to government. The list of current and recent Trilateral Commission members includes not only the corporate captains from the largest corporations on the planet, but also political leaders from both parties: Dick Cheney, Bill Clinton, Dianne Feinstein, Charles Wrangl, Paul Wolfowitz, John D. Rockefeller, and many more political leaders are or were members. Democrat and Republican, they all serve the interests of a global elite, of which they are part.

Third, the age of "free trade" emerged in the 1990s with the establishment of NAFTA, the EU common market, and most importantly, the World Trade Organization (WTO). These organizations establish a framework for the governance of world trade, and can be thought of as world government for the global economy. The problem is that the people who negotiated them are the same elites with the same interests and economic and political power as the Trilateral Commission and Bretton Woods. There is no representation of the people, and the right of the people to self-govern are limited under WTO treaties. Here is an excerpt, attempting to be benign, from the WTO web page:[106]

> At the heart of the system — known as the multilateral trad-ing system — are the WTO's agreements, negotiated and signed by a large majority of the world's trading nations, and ratified in their parliaments. These agreements are the legal ground-rules for international commerce. Essentially, they are contracts, guaranteeing member countries impor-tant trade rights. They also bind governments to keep their trade policies within agreed limits to everybody's benefit.

Reread that last sentence: "They also bind governments to keep their trade policies within agreed limits ..." In liberal democra-cies, that is an erosion of liberty because it means the people cannot change the rules. Environmental, labor, human rights, and other standards that arise from the concerns of the common citizen are forbidden or usually struck down by WTO if they conflict with the movement of capital and trade that serves the interest of corporate elites. Only the elites on the WTO committees can change the rules. There is no labor representation. There is no middle class rep-resentation. There is only capital and the interests of capital. For America, the result is a profound loss of sovereignty and the ability to self-rule through democracy.

In all three stages, the critical observation is that the partic-ipants are the global elites, most of whom represent corporate interests, and their power and intrusion on national sovereignty increases. These institutions are a way to achieve outcomes that the people with the elite interests could not achieve legislatively. Only in what is becoming world economic government will Americans apparently stand for unelected people to establish the laws under which we live, enforce those laws, and adjudicate disputes. In world economic governance, the three branches of government are one.

---

106 http://www.wto.org/english/thewto_e/whatis_e/inbrief_e/inbr00_e.htm.

Closer to home, the confluence of the two kinds of power on the body politic of America has been significant. The political power gained by corporations through the legal changes, granting of political rights via court decisions, and their sophisticated behavior result in four characteristics of their behavior that are quite common in the business world. Although corruption is and ought to be illegal, secrecy, favoritism, and buying influence through campaign finance can be achieved through legal means. All four affect our government and American citizens, and all four need to be understood.

SECRECY

One trait seems to unite corporations across the board: corporations are secretive and tend to hide too much of their knowledge. To an extent, a certain amount of secrecy is necessary in a competitive economic environment. The competition for knowledge and ideas creates a dynamic vitality that is desirable for an economy. But too often, the legitimate right to trade secrets and proprietary market knowledge erodes into an illegitimate hiding of necessary public information. For years, tobacco companies in the U.S. claimed there was no link between health problems and cigarette smoking. In 1992 investigative reporters uncovered the truth—that these companies knew the link existed and made broad efforts to suppress the information and, in fact, utilized it to increase the addictive power of tobacco. They had known all along exactly that which they publicly denied was knowable. Even the most reserved corporate officer should seriously examine this kind of behavior.

The ability of corporations to be secretive and withhold information raises significant concerns. What does the nuclear power industry know that they are not telling us? Or the makers of the new, more potent pesticides? What do the genetic engineers know about their genetically engineered food crops? What about the oil companies and their true awareness of global warming versus their public denials that it is happening? There are many other examples of this sort of stonewalling of information, from Dow-Corning knowingly selling dangerous silicone breast implants, to the A. J. Robbins Company's Dalkon Shield and Merck's Vioxx. Once society has granted the privilege of incorporation, the companies hide the knowledge society requires in order to better serve its needs.

Dangerous and problematic, corporate secrecy inhibits the protection of liberty. Citizens are forced to make choices without knowing the possible impact on their lives, liberty, and pursuit of happiness. Free market dogma argues that corporate freedom and individual freedom go hand-in-hand. But this argument conceals a problem: no one can credibly argue that we are more free when we know less about the dangers to us and the impact of our decisions on our own lives and of those around us.

CORRUPTION

Secrecy seems inevitably to lead to corruption. For example, Vice President Cheney's secret Energy Task Force met behind closed doors, discussed privately the energy policy for the entire country, and excluded many parties with serious interests in the issue, such as alternative energy companies and environmental organizations. Thanks to a Supreme Court ruling protecting those proceedings, we will never know their content. But we know the impact: a $14 billion taxpayer giveaway to energy companies focused on oil, gas, and coal, where record profits are being made as the president signs the bill; a war in Iraq which serves the long-term interests of the oil companies; and no governmental leadership in alternative power sources, energy independence, or environmental stewardship.

Corruption has indeed been raised to brazen new levels of refinement by the Bush administration. Republican government officials must remember the $20 million ranch given to President Reagan after he left office as a "gift" from corporate supporters. Many officials have their own interests in corporate outcomes, some of which are obvious, others less so. Such officials commit outrageous crimes against the American people by bending the public trust to their own benefit. Here is a brief but all-too-familiar sampling:

- At the start of the Iraq War, Halliburton received an open-ended, uncontested contract to provide services to the government for ten years *with no cap on spending*. Vice President Cheney still received direct payments from Halliburton as late as January 2005.

- The Coalition Provisional Authority of the Iraq War has been documented as missing—unaccounted for—$8.8 billion in taxpayer money. The government shows little or no interest in investigating. L. Paul Bremer, the head of the CPA at the time, excuses it as a confusing situation.

- Tom DeLay built the so-called K-street project to enrich himself, Republicans, and his lobbying and corporate friends at the public trough. Disgraced lobbyist Jack Abramoff was a friend and confidant of DeLay's, visited with Bush at the White House on many occasions, and sold his access and influence to almost anyone who would pay for it. Abramoff's influence was gained by getting others to send DeLay, Ohio Representative Bob Ney, and probably additional people on golf junkets and other trips.

Critics will no doubt point out that corruption and self-dealing are not limited to any one party. They are correct. Ethical issues damaged the careers of Jim Wright, Dan Rostenkowski, and Bill Clinton, as well as many Republicans. But the few examples given above illustrate egregious corruption that is fueled by corporate power and which reflect the current state of governmental corruption. They reflect the increasing corruption of public policy enabled by the abuse of corporate power.

FAVORITISM

Favoritism refers to the less obvious kinds of access which provide corporations with undue influence in the legislative process. Rather than tending to the people's business, government officials support particular corporate interests over those of the country, which results in awarding windfalls to the favored few at the expense of the general public.

Here are a few examples:

- **Media Concentration:** In June 2003, the FCC changed its rules to expand media consolidation. The new rules enable corporations to own up to 90 percent of the television stations, enormous numbers of radio stations, and cross-own television, radio and print media. As a result, a few corporations control a very large portion of the public airwaves. In return, FCC officials have enjoyed $2.8 million in travel and entertainment expenses paid for by the broadcast and telecommunications industries.[107] Corporations favoring the Bush agenda were best positioned to take advantage of the new deregulation.

- **Bankruptcy Law:** In April 2005, Republicans forced through Congress—and President Bush signed—a new bankruptcy law virtually written by the credit card companies. The bill makes it much harder for ordinary Americans to file for bankruptcy protection, provides asset protection only for the very wealthy, and makes it easier for corporations to file for bankruptcy.

- **Drug Company Giveaway:** In 2003, Medicare Part D legislation included a provision outlawing government officials from negotiating prices with drug companies. Why would the government outlaw negotiation except to increase payments to those companies? In June 2006—shortly after implementation of Part D—new studies showed a general increase in drug prices.

- **Energy Company Giveaway:** The energy bill President Bush has been pushing for four years was finally passed by the Republican-controlled Congress, which releases $14 billion in subsidies to oil and gas companies, who are already making enormous profits. The excuse: stimulate more production—as if oil at $70 per barrel is not incentive enough.

---

107 Williams, Bob and Morgan Jindrich. "On the Road Again—and Again, Report for The Center for Public Integrity." http://www.openairwaves.org/telecom/report.aspx?aid=15.

Favoritism can become theft—theft of public, taxpayer dollars for the benefit of private corporate interests—masquerading as policy. Even worse, the theft being perpetrated by the current administration is theft of money the government does not have; it is borrowed money. The benefit is swallowed up by corporations, and the liability is passed on to the general public and subsequent generations.

CAMPAIGN FINANCE

Corporate misbehavior comes full circle in the world of campaign finance where corporations and their incredible wealth buy access and influence by contributing to the campaigns, parties, PACs and 521s of their favorite candidates. Most corporations make contributions to candidates on both sides in order to secure influence, although most weight their contributions in favor of one side or the other. During the 2000 election debacle—which gave us a glimpse of things to come—the line between the corporations and government was severely blurred. George W. Bush and his entourage were flown around the country, to and from Florida and elsewhere, on the jet planes of Enron Corporation and Ken Lay, Enron's former Chairman. Political attack ad campaigns are primarily funded by the donations of corporate players, wealthy people who derive their money from corporate operations and ownership. These examples illustrate undue influence on the political process by corporate power and money.

A FEW THINGS THAT WILL NOT WORK TO CONTROL CORPORATE POWER

Given all these problems, thoughtful progressives, moderates, and conservatives have floated ideas on what to do. Here are a few of them that are unlikely to work.

Any attempt to rein in the burgeoning corporate power will surely raise the free-marketer's cry, "Let the markets decide!" This is a red herring. Markets do not, cannot, and never have determined behavior. They don't even determine value very well, as Warren Buffett and other great stock market investors have proven. They do accomplish one thing very well: markets determine price based on supply and demand. They do that well; but that is all they do.

It is disingenuous or uninformed to argue that the market controls behavior. Certainly, wise leaders will avoid bad publicity which matters to their customer base, but markets do not control behavior. Markets alone cannot stop market domination, monopolization, oligopoly, red-lining, and other unjust practices. Markets cannot stop unfair labor practices, consolidation that eliminates competitive technologies, or environmental destruction. They are not designed to do that. Markets set prices; that is it. To claim anything else is folly, sham, or an outright lie.

Similarly, it is folly to rely on corporate leaders to be "responsible." As the examples of Bill Norris and Warren Anderson showed, the conflicts of interest are too profound, and the legal responsibilities of leaders are weighted against social responsibility. The problem is not one of individual integrity; it is a structural issue of the corporate entity itself.

In the 1990s, Charles Sykes blamed therapists for this lack of accountability[108] and Amitai Etzioni blamed affirmative action for the cultural crisis in responsibility in America.[109] In the twenty-first century, Ann Coulter, Rush Limbaugh, and Jerry Falwell blame "liberals."[110] And yet, if corporations can't be held responsible for toxic dumps, poisoned waters, dirty air, bad drugs, financial mismanagement, and communities destroyed by unemployment, why should individuals take responsibility for their communities, for the waters, for using the products they buy properly and wisely for their families? A call for personal responsibility is disingenuous in

---

108 Sykes, Charles. *A Nation of Victims*. St. Martin's Press, New York, 1992.

109 Etzioni, Amitai. *The Spirit of Community*. Crown Publishers, New York, 1993.

110 For example, see books by these authors including: Coulter, Ann. *Treason*. Crown Forum, New York, 2003 and *High Crimes and Misdemeanors*. Regenery Publishing, Washington, DC, 1998. Hawken, Paul. *The Ecology of Commerce*. Harper Business, Division of Harper Collins, New York, 1993.

the absence of a call for corporate structure reform that finally holds corporate people accountable for their corporate actions.[111]

On the other hand, many progressives have argued for an end to the doctrine of corporate personhood.[112] Terminate corporate personhood and all the rights assigned to corporations eventually disintegrate because the foundation of those rights crumbles. It is a tempting notion, but there are three problems with this approach. First, it is highly unlikely to succeed, given the long legal precedent for the doctrine and the enormous power entrenched against such a move. Even if it could be successful, it would take a very long time; over one hundred years were required to create the precedent, and an additional one hundred years have reinforced it. It will not be quickly reversed.

Second, the ramifications of changing the doctrine are unpredictable. The termination of the doctrine, if done without proper care, could be used to provide more power to corporate structures rather than less. Given the current imbalance of political power based on money and the recent experience of so-called free trade negotiations and treaties, the likelihood of such influence on a major piece of legal doctrine and resulting regulations seems substantial.

Third, the corporate sector and global elites have successfully transformed the global economy through the free trade treaties. Nationality matters less to corporate operations now than ever, with the result being that threats to their rights could be met with migration out of America. The results of a mass move of corporations on this basis, even if it is only a legal maneuver, remain unclear.

From the conservative call to let the markets decide to the progressive call to end the doctrine of corporate personhood, most

---

111   In the wake of the Enron, WorldCom, and Adelphia scandals, Congress passed the Sarbanes-Oxley law which strengthens accountability for corporate reporting. Sarbanes-Oxley is a necessary step to protect investors, and it is an attempt to hold executives accountable for their actions. But its scope is strictly limited.

112   See for example http://www.reclaimdemocracy.org, http://www.spiritone.com, http://www.ratical.org, and http://www.mcn.org/e/iii/afd/santaclara.html.

suggested solutions do not meet the challenge of preserving liberty while maintaining the important power of corporations to energize economic creativity. It is our freedom that is most at stake, and while these solutions leave much to be desired, there are things we can do.

CORPORATE BEHAVIOR

America has clearly chosen to engage the enormous positive power of the corporation as an economic tool. Now, we need to realize that we let that power go too far. We want the benefits, but we need to act to avoid the tremendous risks undertaken as a result of the concentration of power occurring within corporate structures.

Lacking inherent structural controls over the power of corporations that will limit their activities, and lacking the legal framework which enables society to govern corporations differently from individuals, we have only three ways to directly affect corporate behavior: regulation, established political tone, and incentives. As a people, we must exercise these powers, or we risk losing control of our own government. But we must exercise them in such a way that our actions are consistent with progressive, moderate, and conservative modalities of liberalism.

REGULATION

Regulation was the primary twentieth century tool for controlling corporate behavior. Corporate abuses at the beginning of the century were so appalling that regulation was the only way to remedy the situation. Presidents Theodore Roosevelt and Franklin Delano Roosevelt each used regulatory action to confront corporate power. Some of the results included labor standards, minimum wages, health and safety standards, and anti-trust laws. Later in the century, Presidents from both parties instituted environmental regulation, financial reporting, banking regulation, and other areas of regulation. Regulation was central to controlling the abuses of unbridled corporate power and market domination, which were detrimental to the country; progressives, moderates, and conservatives all participated in many of these laws against the forces of domination. Liberalism—corporations notwithstanding—attempts to level the playing field and provide equal opportunity to as many people as possible.

As in all efforts with important good intentions, regulation sometimes created absurd unintended outcomes. Examples include an environmental law which halted a development because of an isolated butterfly species, minimum wage laws that increase the cost of childcare beyond the means of the working poor, transportation regulations that disallow company expansion to certain routes even though they could better serve those routes, and OSHA (Occupational Safety and Health Administration) rules which shut down a factory for having a railing forty inches high instead of forty-two inches high. Such examples are fodder for the right wing, and they were seized upon by the right wing starting mid-century to develop well-publicized arguments against regulation. Ronald Reagan heard the call in the 1980s, and the era of really serious deregulation began.

Yet all these regulations were put in place to address real problems and real inequities of opportunity in the market. Deregulation dogma forgets that. When industries become deregulated, they run amok: one example from the 1990s is the savings and loan industry deregulation, the ensuing collapse and taxpayer financed bail-out, a colossal failure of deregulation.

The Savings & Loan industry began the crucial deregulation in 1980 with the Depository Institutions Deregulation and Monetary Control Act of 1980 (DIDMCA). Key features of the act raised the ceiling for insured accounts from $40,000 to $100,000 and allowed S&Ls to invest in property development themselves.[113] Under the same act, the Federal Home Loan Bank Board was allowed to lower the net worth requirement from 5 percent to 3 per-

---

113   Jameson, Rob. "US Savings & Loan Crisis," Case Study on Erisk website, Sungard Bancware Erisk, 2006. http://www.erisk.com/Learning/CaseStudies/USSavingsLoanCrisis.asp#NOTES.

cent, effectively increasing the leverage of S&Ls and nearly doubling the taxpayer exposure to failure risk.[114] By the mid-1980s, trouble was developing. Accusations of corruption and bribery affected the U.S. Senate (via the infamous "Keating Five"), and the industry began to unravel. While the Federal Savings and Loan Insurance Corporation went insolvent, President George H. W. Bush developed and approved a plan to use taxpayer money to bail out the industry. This action would protect depositors and prevent a run on the S&Ls, but the cost came in at between $125 billion and $190 billion, depending on the source. In today's dollars, that amount would easily exceed the staggering amounts America has spent on the Iraq war. Regulation is a method for preventing these kinds of problems, and when we forget through deregulation, we are prone to repeat our mistakes.

Regulation works, despite the occasional unintended outcome. Before environmental regulation, Lake Erie was dead and the Cuyahoga river was polluted enough to catch fire. Corporations resisted and fought the regulations as "too expensive." But appropriate regulation, ushered in under President Nixon, worked very well. Since regulation, no rivers have burned, and Lake Erie has recovered.

For years car manufacturers resisted putting automatic restraints in vehicles until regulation forced them to do so. The companies have turned the extra costs and features into consumer benefits. From passive seat-belts to the less obtrusive air bag, the market perception of safety—triggered by discussion and debate over the merits of such regulations—has changed dramatically, and car companies now sell cars on the basis of safety records and air bag technology.

Further back in history the unregulated stock market and financial system of the 1920s was a major factor in the Depression. New Deal-era regulation which required honest reporting of trans-

---

114   Jameson, Rob. "US Savings & Loan Crisis," Case Study on Erisk website, Sungard Bancware Erisk, 2006. http://www.erisk.com/Learning/CaseStudies/USSavingsLoanCrisis.asp#NOTES.

actions, separation between banking, investment, and insurance functions, and similar measures played an enormous part in establishing the financial conditions which facilitated the explosive economic growth America enjoyed for most of the ensuing sixty years. The confidence among investors, bankers and borrowers that they were looking at the true picture—what is called "transparency"—enabled the investment boom.

Until now, regulation is and has been an effective tool for affecting and controlling corporate behavior. But the power to regulate is being undermined by three important factors:

- **Right-wing Dogma:** Right-wing dogma like "let the markets decide" and "we can police ourselves" spearhead the arguments against regulation. Behind these one-liners, related anecdotal stories sound unreasonable. The combination works in an electorate where the benefits of regulation—safe work places, labor rights, clean lakes and rivers—are taken for granted because the problems have faded from memory. Because we forget how corporations used to behave before regulation, this popular right-wing dogma holds political sway.

- **Free Trade Agreements:** Free trade agreements undermine the ability of national and local governments to regulate critical issues within their borders. Pollution control, labor laws, quality standards, and many other issues normally reserved to the sovereignty of nations are stipulated in free trade agreements. If a local government were to try to address these issues, the local ordinances might be deemed in violation of the international treaty and therefore nullified. Such nullifications are rare; the real problem is far more subtle because the mere existence of the stipulations changes the local debate. When state and local governments seek to pass regulations, the scope of NAFTA (North American Free Trade Agreement) limitations on the issues set the boundaries of the debate. All issues and solutions which would violate NAFTA are automatically taken off the table. Without even saying the word "regulation," NAFTA guts the regulatory tool. NAFTA, CAFTA (Central American Free Trade

Agreement) and the WTO (World Trade Organization) all share this anti-democratic, anti-local control aspect.

- **Globalization:** Global corporations are increasingly moving operations outside of the national regulatory arena by relocating production far away from their end markets. Whether through organizing off-shore tax havens or moving production to places which are regulation-free, global corporations are taking advantage of the national government's inability to regulate them.

Regulation works, but the regulatory function is under assault by the right wing and the global legal structure for "free trade." Regulation is a tool we need. It can and does change corporate behavior. Regulation stops abuses, limits power, and defines a competitive playing field for all participants.

POLITICAL TONE

Political tone refers to the rhetorical power to change people's attitudes toward the problems we confront. Compare the tone initiated by Bill Clinton in his first term to that developed by George W. Bush after 9/11. In the early 1990s, America was confronting towering deficit spending and debt. Something had to be done. Although it was important to control government growth, that alone could not close the gap. The country needed revenue. For about a year after Clinton was elected to office, two words defined the political tone of our talk: *shared sacrifice*. I remember hearing corporate leaders on radio talk shows discussing the need for shared sacrifice; they were prepared to do their part, and they knew that meant increased taxes for the benefit of the country. Corporate leaders acceded to the direction of political leadership, as they generally do.

Fast forward to the George W. Bush administration. What's their post-9/11 mantra? *Keep buying. Go shopping.* Notice the difference in tone: virtually all of America did. And how has corporate America responded? *Get what you can while the getting is good.* Eliminate the power of the government to negotiate with us (drug bill), demand open-ended, un-capped contracts (Halliburton) and screw the people with bad luck and no health insurance (the bankruptcy law). The mood is one of getting what you can and consolidating power.

The contrast reveals the power of the presidency as a bully pulpit. The president establishes the leadership tone in the country, particularly in regard to corporate behavior. The acceptability and unacceptability of actions matter, and the president establishes the general expectations for corporate behavior from the bully pulpit. Nothing in the political tone set by the president is likely to change the behavior of corporations at the extremes; there will always be corporate do-gooders and corporate crooks. It is the general direction of those in the middle—the vast majority of corporations which is swayed by the political tone set in Washington.

INCENTIVES: TAXES AND SUBSIDIES

The third method for controlling corporate behavior in the interest of the people is through incentives: punitive tax policies, tax breaks, and actual direct subsidy. These work because they, more than other methods, directly speak the language of the corporation: profit. Substantial incentives alter corporate behavior. Reagan's tax reform act of 1986 completely changed the way losses in real estate could be used to shelter income for tax purposes. The act dramatically changed the incentive to build office buildings. Investors stopped financing office building construction, and in a few years the commercial real estate market changed completely. Jimmy Carter's administration provided incentives in the form of substantial tax breaks to individuals and businesses in the solar energy field and that industry flourished. The abolition of those tax breaks under Reagan virtually bankrupted the industry. Incentives represent pure financial logic in terms of corporate behavior. Corporations will change in response to incentives because there is an opportunity to profit. Proper incentives align corporate behavior as well as any other organization with societal goals.

Government inevitably affects the behavior of corporations.

Governmental actions and attitude either move the general corporate mood and behavior toward the public good, or toward detached self-interest. The right-wing dogma—that government has no role affecting corporate behavior—is a delusion; government is always involved. Its actions, inactions, and attitude affect corporate behavior in all situations. The only question is in what way government will affect corporate behavior.

THINGS TO REMEMBER

- Corporations are unique: they never die a natural death, they protect owners from liability for their actions, and they enable the aggregation of wealth and capital.
- Corporations are unique entities designed to focus on the economic sphere. They unleash enormous economic creativity from which society benefits, but they are economically too dominant.
- The corporate expression of political power based on economic power is a reversal of the modern separation of economic, political, and religious spheres.
- The privilege of incorporation demands that society balance the privilege through the expression of its political power.
- Neither free markets nor good people can solve the problems inherent in the corporate structure.
- Liberalism offers three tools which we must use: regulation, political tone, and taxes and incentives.

Renewal of Political Culture

CHAPTER 7

Renewing the Commitment

THE BRIDGE THAT HOLDS THE AMERICAN POLITICAL SPECTRUM together is liberalism. The word belongs to progressives, moderates, and conservatives alike. Liberalism needs the progressive push for fairness and change, the moderate effort toward gradual change and tolerance, and the conservative celebration of long-held principles and careful discipline. America's best solutions and actions are undertaken when all three make real contributions to public policy. While absolutist ideologies close the doors of communication, quality discourse and reason uncover surprising answers to vexing social, economic, religious, and political problems. When we cannot engage in such discourse with clarity and civility, democracy and freedom are minimized. Our challenge is to understand issues, challenges, and problems faced by the country using new cognitive tools outlined in this book.

One new tool is to relate the facts and reality as we know them to the liberal principles of the nation. How does the new policy on torture relate to the Rule of Law or the principle of individual sovereignty? How does the concentration of media serve the Bill of Rights, the Constitution, or the Declaration of Independence? How does one's own position align? Is the argument being made in violation of these basic principles?

For example, when the president expands his power and diminishes congressional oversight, the Constitution is being eroded, perhaps overthrown. We need to see this. When gradual, incremental growth in corporate power unduly influences the political debate in the country, political liberty is losing out to feudal-like corporate forces. Does it matter whether it is viewed from progressive, moderate, or conservative standpoints? The liberal principle is being cast aside. Just by seeing it, we save ourselves from the lie. Comparing current events to liberal principles grounds one in the actual political history of the nation. We will find common ground with most Americans on these principles.

A second tool to help bridge the gap and increase understanding is to analyze ourselves and our opponents. Are you progressive, moderate, or conservative on this issue? What about your opponent? Does your position constitute impossible idealism or rigid moralism? Does your opponent do the same? We can identify where we stand by considering the characteristics of legitimate and illegitimate progressivism, moderatism, and conservatism (see Chapter 1). But also, and just as importantly, we can recognize absolutism of the type that Paul O'Neill recognized in his confrontation with Dick Cheney (see Chapter 1). By identifying these standpoints and positions, we have a significant advantage. We gain a framework for understanding the dynamics of arguments and thereby overcome our common bewilderments and frequent mistakes. Both self-knowledge and knowledge of one's opponent are critical to building the bridge of liberalism. American liberal principles serve us well in conversation or debate with all modalities of liberalism, and when the opponent is arguing from a non-liberal standpoint, we take appropriate action and avoid the mistaken assumption that we share the same goal.

Third, Americans can clarify realm. By knowing that an issue belongs to politics, economics, or religion, we can avoid the confusions and obfuscations so often used by liberalism's opponents going back at least to the fascists of the 1920s and 1930s. When a person argues that a provision of the tax code is immoral, the lines between religion and politics are being blurred. When a corporation is allowed to write a bill that is put before Congress, the lines between economics and politics are being blurred. These are reckless and illegitimate attempts to confuse the distinctions between these realms, and they constitute direct attacks on modern thinking and liberal principle.

Liberals across the spectrum understand these distinctions; they are expressed eloquently in the idea of "separation of church and state." They are expressed less eloquently and less directly in the notion of the corporation, which is set up to free itself from considering its impact on society. When issues are debated within the realm to which they belong, the hot emotional energy of absolutism is displaced by reason and thought; i.e., the issue can be decided on the merits. Political decisions can be made on the basis of good pubic policy and the actors in that arena. Economic decisions can be made by economic actors and market forces, and religious decisions can be made by the religious community, not by government. At a minimum, we can call into question the point at which a debate is crossing from one realm into the other, so as to determine the tactics being used.

The fourth tool is to recognize and differentiate the two forms of consciousness that relate to feudal and liberal structures: premodern consciousness gives rise to feudal-like structures and ideas, and modern consciousness gives rise to liberal structures and ideas. This is critical for determining communication strategies with all Americans. A liberal engagement with an issue will be reflected in a discourse of reason and thought, however passionate. A non-liberal engagement will harken to non-liberal principles such as authority, honor-order-duty, and literal religious texts. Morality or idealism will infuse a non-liberal discussion. Recognition that the conversation has moved to a new place can provide an opportunity to change course and improve the dialogue.

. . .

By applying these tools to ourselves and those who disagree with us, we attain a clear awareness of the standpoint from which we speak and on which they stand. It is crucial that the American people begin to see and understand the nature of the debates and discussions which confront us if we are to heal the body politic and adhere to our principles. Progressives too easily and mistakenly interpret real conservatives as right-wingers, and conservatives sometimes mistake progressives for communists or anarchists. These mistakes are the real source of the polarization which infects the body politic. We tend to think it is all caused by the right wing, conspiracy theorists, or someone else. In actuality, our own misunderstanding and misperception live at the root of the divide. Too quickly, we discriminate without knowledge, casting those with a different view into a category where they do not belong. Christian fundamentalists are conflated with neoconservatives and progressives are confused with "liberals." In so doing, the ears close and the conversation stops. The result is that common attitude, "We don't discuss politics; we'd rather keep the peace."

Given these four tools, we can overcome the confusion that intensifies the divide. We can counter it with awareness, see the tactics for the manipulations that they are, and examine our own participation in the political-cultural split which so many Americans abhor. I hope we will see not only that some players in our political life lie outside the spectrum of the American spirit, but also that each of us has participated in the split, the polarization, and the demonization of the other side. With new awareness, we can avoid repeating those errors.

However, our private conversations and debates are not the only place our political life occurs. We face real issues. Liberal religion, economics, and politics are all being passively eroded, if not directly attacked. Seeing this, we also need real, concrete proposals that will stop the erosion if enacted. Following are a few of my ideas for addressing the roots of economic, political, and religious vitality in the America of the early twenty-first century.

FREE AND FAIR ELECTIONS AMENDMENT

One example of a political initiative which serves progressive, moderate, and conservative modalities is my proposal for a Free and Fair Elections Amendment. The integrity of elections stands at the heart of American democracy. The presidential elections of 2000 and 2004 created serious questions about this integrity. Unprecedented discrepancies between exit poll results and election results raised a red flag. Why did exit poll results—exemplifying the most accurate of polling methods—and election results differ? Did exit polling technology get worse? Or did something happen to the integrity of the electoral process?

The resulting spin has focused the public on exit polls. But the significant changes in the system occurred in how we administer elections: electronic voting machines, absentee balloting, and verification of voters all changed. Much attention has centered on electronic voting machine problems.[115] Repeatedly, stories indicated that voters selected one candidate and then were asked to confirm their vote for a different candidate. It is a troubling fact that the machines cannot be audited in terms of who had access to the machines and their data or when they had such access; no paper trail exists for a confirmation count of votes and there is no way for the voter to ensure his or her vote is being cast and counted for the candidates of his or her choice. Computer security experts are appalled by the machines' flaws and how susceptible they are to corruption of data.

With our collective attention drawn to exit poll accuracy, the real debate over electronic voting is locked in a tit-for-tat discussion of details most Americans do not really care about, nor should they. The legitimate concern is that every voting machine should work, count votes accurately, and be auditable and verifiable by hand count, if necessary. Anything less thwarts the will of the people. In a liberal democracy, the will of the people as expressed on election day is of paramount importance.

Although problems in the presidential election in Ohio and a few other states have garnered the most attention, local and state elections in Ohio highlight the real problem. Ballot initiatives that enjoyed nearly two to one public support in polls went down to defeat in November 2005, by nearly the exact reverse margin,

---

115   See a multitude of writings at http://www.freepress.org, http://www
     .uscountvotes.org, and http://www.blackboxvoting.org.

even though there was no measurable change in voter attitudes. Fraud and tampering are the only reasonable explanations. In May 2006, similar election surprises occurred in Cleveland and Cuyahoga County. Voters in these elections are outraged. Security checks of the voting machines continue to turn up the most rudimentary lapses. Salespeople for Diebold—the company manufacturing voting machines—deceived elections boards across the country by claiming their machines were secure and could not be tampered with; later demonstrations proved such tampering was quick, simple, and undetectable. As the truth is coming out, some of those local and state governments are suing Diebold. The company's CEO was forced to resign after his actions became untenable to stockholders. The will of the people is being left in the ash heap of a burning desire to profit from controlled elections on the part of the right wing, putting our very democracy at risk.

While the bickering on technical issues continues unabated—apparently unaffected by facts and hard information—it is precisely the will of the people that is being flouted. There is widespread gnashing of teeth over new laws, accusations of fraud and the legitimacy of President Bush's election. I suggest that citizens go to the core of the problem: pass a "Free and Fair Elections Amendment." The amendment to the constitution would read thus:

> A well regulated election, being necessary to the security of a free state, the right of the people to an audited, voter-verified, certified paper record of the vote, shall not be infringed.[116]

This amendment is important for several reasons. First, the wording offers a clear, direct requirement guiding elections and any counting machines or other technology used to count and assemble votes. It should be election doctrine since it lies at the very heart

---

116 With attorney Robert Hill I drafted and re-drafted the wording of this amendment.

of our democracy and governmental legitimacy. Liberal principle requires such an amendment in the face of the current technological changes. Who will vote against the Free and Fair Elections Amendment? No one who values democracy. An accurate, verifiable count of votes is fundamental to democracy—there's no room to equivocate. To oppose this amendment is to subvert the will of the people. Opposition comes only from people who have narrow interests and narrow arguments, or who are corrupt. Right-wing opponents in the Ohio house passed electronic voting laws that would outlaw any requirement for auditability or paper trails in voting machines. Yet the right of citizens to know who actually won, and confidence in the accurate counting of votes is very difficult to oppose. This amendment puts liberal principle squarely back into the center of our political debate.

Second, this amendment has widespread ramifications. It would affect the design and implementation of voting machines and electoral processes in every federal, state, and local election. It would thwart those who want to concentrate power in an elite group at the top of the right-wing chart, and move power back into the hands of the people. It would ensure that local officials and states live up to consistent constitutional standards, and it would prevent end runs by politically-chosen partisan boards, legislatures, or secretaries of state.

Third, the Fair and Free Elections Amendment focuses the attention of the electorate—and the debate in the body politic—on the real issue: the integrity of every vote. Constitutional amendments usually take a long time to pass. Congress votes on it, and three-fourths of the states have to ratify it. This process can take a decade, long enough to provoke debate throughout our democracy on the integrity of the voting and elections system. This can only be a good thing for democracy and liberal principle.

Fourth, it is nonpartisan. Democrats, Republicans, Greens, and Independents all have a stake in the proper counting of votes. So do progressives, moderates, and conservatives. Not only does the very legitimacy of government depend on it, but so does party funding, recognition of status as major parties, and a clear picture of where the parties actually stand in the body politic. The only logical reason to oppose such an amendment is because your own power position relies on the corruption of the system. Diebold may not support it because—as some believe—the company has built in a method for adjusting elections, or because it is unprofitable to incur the cost of securing their systems to the standards which the amendment would require. Either way, their opposition is based on their power interest. Not even Diebold can legitimately claim that the lack of such security and verifiability is in the interest of democracy.

The Free and Fair Elections Amendment, as I have proposed it, can and should be taken up in every state and in the Congress. It is an example of a political move that should appeal to all three modalities of American liberalism.

PAY FOR THE WAR

If the country is going to engage in a war, then the country ought to pay for it. At the time of this writing, the cost of the wars in Iraq and Afghanistan is a combined $275 billion. It is expected to go to at least $400 billion before it is over, and there is little sign of the American involvement ending any time soon. The cost could easily hit half a trillion dollars by the time we actually leave Iraq.

While the cost is enormous, the travesty is that we are not paying for it: we are borrowing for it. At a minimum we should pass a temporary war tax to pay for the war. The war tax would come from those who have enjoyed the deepest tax cuts of recent years: the very wealthy with very high incomes. The exorbitant borrowing driven by the war is compromising our economic well-being by undermining our fiscal well-being. The borrowing is unsustainable, inflationary, and economically de-stabilizing.

Fiscal responsibility in this case lines up with the interests of progressives, moderates, and conservatives. Traditionally, true conservatives have been the guardians of government fiscal responsibility. The reckless financial governance of our military spending illustrates just how much true conservative concerns have been sidelined by the Bush administration. Moderate interests are served by bringing a halt to policies that are likely to destabilize the economy. Progressive values would be reflected in the progressiveness of the tax. And all are served by automatic cancellation of the tax when the war costs are completely paid for.

ENTREPRENEURSHIP

Entrepreneurs are the creative engine of the American economy, living the liberal promise to pursue happiness and economic liberty on their own terms. Entrepreneurs create new products and services, manufacture them with new technologies, and market them in innovative ways. Entrepreneurs live on the leading edge of the liberal free enterprise system, and the small businesses which they create are central to the American middle class.

The 2005 bankruptcy law, written by huge corporate credit card companies, passed by the Republican Congress, and signed by President Bush, has been roundly decried as an attack on people down on their luck. Nearly half of all bankruptcies result from medically-related expenses or from divorce or death in the family. Apparently the credit card companies and their congressional friends believe that such people should not be entitled to relief in bankruptcy. If you are down on your luck those companies believe you must be forced to pay every penny of their 30 percent APR interest charges. To many people, this is an outrage.

The hidden impact is that the new law dampens economic creativity by increasing the risk to entrepreneurs. The entrepreneur and small business press is full of stories about start-ups funded with credit cards, even at high interest rates; for many small businesses it is the only way to get initial funding.[117] Whether through credit cards, bank debt, home equity loans, or any other borrowed funds, entrepreneurs always face the prospect of the new enterprise failing; and they never face it lightly. Even under the old laws, one did not seek bankruptcy. Yet to know there is a way out—albeit nasty

---

117 Read almost any issue of *Inc.* or *Entrepreneur* magazines for examples.

and undesirable—provides many entrepreneurs with that extra little daring to take the risk. The risk equation has changed substantially under the new bankruptcy law; inevitably, it will dampen entrepreneurial activity.

Under the old law there was a balance between society's interest in holding people accountable and its desire to foster economic creativity, a balance which is now gone. The effects have not been immediately noticeable in the short run. Years from now we will look back at the statistics and see a decrease in small business development, a decrease in employment in small businesses and a decrease in the vigor of the real economy in which most middle class people work. While a few businesses may close, the real problem will be in the many businesses which do not open as a result of this law.

To again liberate economic creativity and ensure the vibrancy of our small business community, the new bankruptcy law should be repealed and replaced with the old one. Our ability to respond to the challenges of tomorrow is at stake. New energy technologies will not come from Exxon, but from the entrepreneurs. New transportation solutions will come from entrepreneurs. New cures for disease, new diagnostic tools, new computer technologies, nano-technologies, and new agricultural methods are all being developed by entrepreneurs. Large, established companies generally have a disincentive to develop new technologies because they are heavily invested in old ones from which they want to receive the highest possible return. Developing new technologies with better answers to our problems is not in the interest of large companies because they make the older technologies and methods obsolete and eventually worthless. A vibrant small business community is nothing less than our collective ability to respond creatively to society's needs, challenges, and desires. In a world confronting global warming, globalization, abject poverty, and many other problems, this creativity is essential to our well-being.

THE DIGNITY OF LABOR

While entrepreneurs have only recently come under attack, labor has been under attack for decades. The most recent assault started in the 1980s when Ronald Reagan broke up PATCO—the Professional Air Traffic Controllers Organization. Reagan's confrontation with and victory over PATCO signaled to corporations that the government would support their efforts to fight the power of labor unions. Government now abandoned the sense of even-handedness between labor and capital, and would work definitively on the side of capital.

Since that time, many major government initiatives have done exactly that, culminating in George W. Bush's so-called "ownership society." The defeat of PATCO, the 1986 tax reform act, NAFTA and WTO agreements, the subsidization of jobs outsourced to China and India, the gutting of the National Labor Relations Board, and the cuts in OSHA and other worker safety administration enforcement capabilities all indicate labor is under attack. Mine workers have been left to die in mines which have been cited for safety violations over two hundred times in the past few years. Nothing was done to address the violations, men died because of this neglect, and the company and the government seem to be saying, "That's too bad."

The attack on labor must be reversed. Working men and women deserve dignity for the work they do. We must challenge our traditional views of labor, and not just the manufacturing and service-worker unions, which are critical and most directly under attack. As software engineers have begun to discover, their jobs can be easily outsourced, and that move is coming from the same lack of respect for work. Professionals like doctors and white collar workers in young firms are required to sleep at work and exhaust themselves with travel while their families grow up without them. Unions fought the battle of the ten- and twelve-hour work day decades ago.

What does this really mean? It means the people are under attack by a government serving corporate and capital interests. Herein is one accurate barometer of democracy. Even though we routinely vote, the people are not governing themselves. The people have not demanded lower worker safety standards, lower paying jobs, or the elimination of the middle class. These policies serve corporate interests, not the people's interests. We are going in exactly the opposite direction we should be going in order to build an American liberal economy.

The United States should be the world leader in setting high standards for treatment of workers, environmental standards, and the entrepreneurial economy. We should be setting the very highest standards and demanding that other nations who want to trade with us achieve the same high standards. There are several areas in which we need to start refocusing on workers and the middle class:

- Stop subsidizing the outsourcing of jobs and the movement of facilities overseas. This is a ludicrous policy.

- Increase worker safety standards and fully fund the enforcement of those standards, whichever agency is in charge.

- Change *all* international trade agreements to demand that American trading partners rise to the same levels of worker safety and dignity, environmental protection, and entrepreneurial development as the U.S. as a *pre-condition* to trade with us.

These ideas will help to restore the dignity to labor, and they transform American prosperity into a force for good in the world. They say we value workers, people, and the middle class, and they align the principles of liberalism with those values.

RELIGIOUS RENEWAL

In the religious sphere American liberalism expresses itself in the same three modalities: progressive, moderate, and conservative. On the conservative side the danger is that it is easy to slip into fundamentalism, which may present itself as conservative but is really a radical extreme. The danger on the progressive side is radical atheism, a sort of literalist secularism which denies the empirical reality of other people's spiritual experiences, and the danger in the moderate approach is radical disengagement from religion and spirit while going through the motions of church attendance. All three possibilities claim a singular truth unto themselves amounting to dissociation from the core of liberal humanity. None serves liberalism.

Two writers who understand the problem faced in religion are Jim Wallis, author of *God's Politics*,[118] and Michael Lerner, author of *The Left Hand of God*.[119] Wallis is an evangelical who distances himself from the mean-spirited fundamentalist theology and truly reads the Gospels and asks, "To what are worshippers called?" The essence of Wallis's book is captured in the questions he asks as subtitles to three parts of the book:

* When did Jesus become Pro-War?
* When did Jesus become Pro-Rich?
* When did Jesus become a selective moralist?

Many progressives have asked similar questions, but many progressives are not practicing evangelicals. Their questions and challenges fall flat as apparently disingenuous efforts to skewer the faith. Wallis cannot be discounted that way. He is an evangelical, the editor of *Sojourners*, and the leader of faith-based initiatives to end poverty in America. Wallis and others like him need to be read carefully, discussed, and debated in order to better inform our experience of faith, whatever its source may be. We must entertain the legitimate notion of progressive evangelicals, and be ready to engage such a new possibility.

Rabbi Michael Lerner, editor of *Tikkun* magazine, offered an insightful assessment from another angle of the spiritual dilemma facing America today. He approached the problem from the viewpoint of a social scientist, including interviews, surveys, and other data collection techniques. His goal was to capture a picture of the spiritual situation in America today, and what he found is evidence of a spiritual crisis: people who have everything, whose basic needs

---

118 Wallis, Jim. *God's Politics*. Harper San Francisco, Division of Harper Collins, New York, 2005.

119 Lerner, Michael. *The Left Hand of God*. Harper San Francisco, Division of Harper Collins, New York, 2006.

are met, yet still yearn for some deeper experience of life. No matter what our material satisfactions may be, Lerner finds the American people to be spiritually disaffected. Many people sense it vaguely but can't clearly articulate it.

According to Lerner, the Christian fundamentalists have capitalized on this longing and emptiness. Mainstream churches have too often failed the people, and right-wing churches offer something many people find attractive and which seems to respond to that longing and emptiness. Many get involved even though they realize the policies advocated by the church they join are either contrary to their own interests or in opposition to their beliefs. That does not matter for many people because the experience of a relationship with God is very powerful to them and they are willing to put aside these other concerns. Many pro-choice Roman Catholics confront a similar tension in which the value of the faith community and religious practice outweigh differences of opinion on social and political issues. Complete agreement between a church community and its leadership is rare, and discrepancies are a part of any practice of faith.

In many ways Jim Wallis represents a spiritual consciousness which confronts the world honestly. He concludes that God's world is in crisis, and God's people must act to repair it. Michael Lerner starts with the world as it is and concludes from empirical evidence that the culture faces a spiritual crisis. Lerner and Wallis present two perspectives on the same phenomenon: a dissociation between spiritual-religious practice and social practice. Both are calling for a psychological alignment between these powerful forces as an antidote to the dissociation of religion evident in fundamentalism. Such an alignment calls for religion to relate to, rather than dominate, the economic and political, the social and the personal. Alignment and integration serve the liberal American spirit by removing the dissociation.

Wallis and Lerner are two examples of thinkers deep in the traditions of American liberalism. There many others exploring this fertile ground. If one trusts his church to guide him on a journey, the church is a great place to get guidance. But many Americans do not attend church regularly, and many others seek a more objective view of religion and how it operates in our society. Study, thought, and meditation are necessary practices for an initial renewal of religion and spirituality in America.

INDIVIDUAL ACTION

America needs to wake up and get engaged now to protect the liberty and democracy we enjoy. As a people we have grown passive to the commitment liberalism requires of us, and almost ignorant of the world around us.

It is commonplace to recognize that we live in an economy where knowledge is economic power and knowledge workers compete on the basis of what they know. Ubiquitous business ideas like the learning organization or Peter Senge's *Fifth Discipline* rivet the attention of corporate leaders because they recognize the incredible power of knowledge and information. Large organizations are creating a new role called the Chief Learning Officer to express the need for learning and making information accessible.

The power of knowledge applies to more than just the economy. We are actually in a knowledge world where political knowledge will win in politics and religious knowledge will win in religion. Christian fundamentalists wield influence over so many people because of their knowledge of the Bible, and while many mainstream Christians have deep beliefs but less knowledge, they can be susceptible to the fundamentalist arguments. It is not that their faith is shallow, but rather that their knowledge is thin. The same is true for many in politics.

Where individuals are prone to use all means necessary to take power for themselves, one of the primary tools is the lie. We are faced with the outright lies of our political leaders like Donald Rumsfeld, Dick Cheney, and George W. Bush, as well as the lies of business leaders from Enron, Worldcom, and Adelphia. We are faced with the absurd lies deriving from literal readings of biblical passages involving the age of the planet and evolution, and we are faced with the industrial lie that global warming is up for debate.

The lies confuse the citizens, thereby disempowering them. Confusion and disempowerment may be the actual underlying purpose; the lies must stop.

And yet, the effectiveness of the lies is largely our own responsibility. As a people, we have allowed ourselves to lack knowledge and education. In many cases, we lack the most basic knowledge: knowledge of the workings of our government and our rights as expressed in our founding documents; a detailed knowledge of theology and biblical texts; and the knowledge and skills of entrepreneurship, business, and the economic world. This ignorance makes us susceptible to the lies, and when the lies are sophisticated, it is easy to be duped. We cannot afford the luxury of our ignorance anymore.

Undoubtedly, some will see this as a call for better education for our kids, and it certainly is that. But our situation is far more urgent: we need to educate ourselves as adults *now*. *Call to Liberty*, I hope, has provided an introduction to many important aspects of this education. But for those willing to undertake the hard work of learning to preserve and enhance liberty, here are a few ideas.

- **Political Knowledge:** Learn to describe the principles of liberalism and their history; memorize the Bill of Rights, and carefully read the Declaration of Independence, and the U.S. Constitution. If so motivated, continue on with the Federalist Papers and biographies of the founding fathers. Read John Locke, Jean Jacques Rousseau, Edmund Burke, John Stuart Mill, John Maynard Keynes, Friedrich A. Hayek, Immanuel Kant, and Ken Wilber.

- **Economic Knowledge:** Study the history of corporations in America, from railroads to robber baron trusts, to multinationals and global corporations, and the legal structure of corporations. Study entrepreneurship, economic creativity, capital, labor, and goods and services markets. Understand the history of labor and its role in liberty, from indentured servitude and apprenticeships in trades, to slavery, internships, residencies, and professions.

- **Religious Knowledge:** Study the history and theology of Christianity, Judaism, Islam, and Native American and New Age spirituality. These are all part of the American cultural experience, and greater understanding comes from studying all of them. Since Christianity is dominant in the culture, understand Christian principles and biblical principles. Know the commonly quoted biblical verses, and know responses to them.

The joy of engaging liberalism is a fuller freedom for our own lives: more creativity, vitality, and spontaneity. There is also a calm from fulfilling obligations and a sense of purpose derived from participation in a larger story. Self-education and discovery can be a joy. You can start here. A liberal culture will promote this joy, this creativity, and this desire. America has a long tradition of liberal philosophy and ideas which will not fade away quickly. We can bank on that tradition, but it will serve us only if we serve it by engaging the freedom and liberty that are ours. In the end, the founding fathers left us as much responsibility as opportunity with those great words: "... to Life, Liberty, and the Pursuit of Happiness."

The Bill of Rights

Perhaps the first expression of the principles of liberalism which live in the national soul today is found in the Bill of Rights. The Bill of Rights consists of the first ten amendments to the Constitution which were part of brokering the deal between the states to actually establish the federal government. By way of a reminder they are printed here:

AMENDMENT I

Congress shall make no law respecting an establishment of religion, or prohibiting the free exercise thereof; or abridging the freedom of speech, or of the press; or the right of the people peaceably to assemble, and to petition the government for a redress of grievances.

AMENDMENT II

A well regulated militia, being necessary to the security of a free state, the right of the people to keep and bear arms, shall not be infringed.

AMENDMENT III

No soldier shall, in time of peace be quartered in any house, without the consent of the owner, nor in time of war, but in a manner to be prescribed by law.

AMENDMENT IV

The right of the people to be secure in their persons, houses, papers, and effects, against unreasonable searches and seizures, shall not be violated, and no warrants shall issue, but upon probable cause, supported by oath or affirmation, and particularly describing the place to be searched, and the persons or things to be seized.

AMENDMENT V

No person shall be held to answer for a capital, or otherwise infamous crime, unless on a presentment or indictment of a grand jury, except in cases arising in the land or naval forces, or in the militia, when in actual service in time of war or public danger; nor shall any person be subject for the same offense to be twice put in jeopardy of life or limb; nor shall be compelled in any criminal case to be a witness against himself, nor be deprived of life, liberty, or property, without due process of law; nor shall private property be taken for public use, without just compensation.

AMENDMENT VI

In all criminal prosecutions, the accused shall enjoy the right to a speedy and public trial, by an impartial jury of the state and district wherein the crime shall have been committed, which district shall have been previously ascertained by law, and to be informed of the nature and cause of the accusation; to be confronted with the witnesses against him; to have compulsory process for obtaining witnesses in his favor, and to have the assistance of counsel for his defense.

AMENDMENT VII

In suits at common law, where the value in controversy shall exceed twenty dollars, the right of trial by jury shall be preserved, and no fact tried by a jury, shall be otherwise reexamined in any court of the United States, than according to the rules of the common law.

AMENDMENT VIII

Excessive bail shall not be required, nor excessive fines imposed, nor cruel and unusual punishments inflicted.

AMENDMENT IX

The enumeration in the Constitution, of certain rights, shall not be construed to deny or disparage others retained by the people.

AMENDMENT X

The powers not delegated to the United States by the Constitution, nor prohibited by it to the states, are reserved to the states respectively, or to the people.

Bibliography

Armstrong, Karen. Speech, Westminster Town Hall Forum, Minneapolis, 2005.

Bamford, James. *A Pretext for War*. New York: Doubleday, 2004.

Bennett, William (ed).*The Book of Virtues*. New York: Simon & Schuster, 1993.

Berman, Paul. *Terror and Liberalism*. New York-London: W. W. Norton & Company, 2003.

Boot, Max. "Myths about Neoconservatism," in *The Neocon Reader*, edited by Irwin Stelzer. New York: Grove Press, 2004.

Boyte, Harry C. *Everyday Politics*. Philadephia: University of Pennsylvania Press, 2004.

Brock, David. *The Conscience of a Conservative*. New York: Crown Publishers, 2002.

Burke, Jason. *Al Qaeda: Casting a Shadow of Terror*. London: I. B. Tauris, 2003.

Coulter, Ann. *Treason*. New York: Crown Forum, 2003.

Coulter, Ann. *High Crimes and Misdemeanors*. Washington, DC: Regenery Publishing, 1998.

De Soto, Hernando. *The Mystery of Capital*. New York: Basic Books, 2002.

Ellis, Joseph J. *What Did the Declaration Declare?* Boston-New York: Bedford/St. Martin's, 1999.

Etzioni, Amitai. *The Spirit of Community*. New York: Crown Publishers, 1993.

Friedman, Benjamin. *The Moral Consequences of Economic Growth.* New York: Alfred A. Knopf, 2005.

Grant, George. *The Changing of the Guard: Biblical Principles for Political Action.* Middlesex: Dominion Press, 1987.

Greenberg, Karen J. and Joshua L Dratel (eds). *The Torture Papers: The Road to Abu Ghraib,* New York: Cambridge University Press, 2005.

Hagerty, Barbara Bradley. "Religious Schools Train Lawyers for Culture Wars," *National Public Radio,* May 6, 2005.

Handy, Robert T. *A History of the Churches in the United States and Canada.* Oxford-New York-Toronto-Melbourne: Oxford University Press, 1976.

Hayek, Friedrich A. *The Road to Serfdom.* Chicago: University of Chicago Press, 1944.

Hersch, Seymour M. "The Iran Plans: Would President Bush go to War to Stop Iran from Getting the Bomb?" *New Yorker,* April 17, 2006.

Hawken, Paul. *The Ecology of Commerce.* New York: Harper Business, Division of Harper Collins, 1993.

Korten, David. *The Post-Corporate World, Life After Capitalism.* San Francisco: Berrett-Koehler Publishers and Kuhmarian Press, 1999.

Lappe, Frances Moore. *Food First.* San Francisco, 1977.

Lerner, Michael. *The Left Hand of God.* New York: Harper San Francisco, Division of Harper Collins, 2006.

Lindsay, Thomas M. *A History of the Reformation.* New York: Charles Scribner's Sons, 1916.

Mander, Jerry. *In the Absence of the Sacred.* San Francisco: Sierra Club Books, 1992.

Pringle, Heather. *The Master Plan: Himmler's Scholars and the Holocaust.* New York: Hyperion, 2006.

A Report of the Project for the New American Century. Washington, DC, 2000.

Roy, Olivier. *Globalized Islam.* New York: Columbia University Press, 2004.

Rumsfeld, Donald. Speech to American Legion, September 2006.

Scheuer, Michael. (First published as by "Anonymous"). *Imperial Hubris: Why the West Is Losing the War on Terror.* Washington, DC: Brassey's Inc., 2004.

Smith, Adam. *An Inquiry into the Nature and Causes of The Wealth of Nations.* Edinburgh, 1776.

Snell, Bradford C. *Statement of Bradford C. Snell before the United States Senate Subcommittee on Antitrust and Monopoly: Presented at hearings on the ground transportation ... in connection with S1167,* February 26, 1974.

Steinfels, Peter. *The Neoconservatives.* New York: Simon & Schuster, 1979.

Suskind, Ron. *The Price of Loyalty.* New York: Simon & Schuster, 2004.

Sykes, Charles. *A Nation of Victims.* New York: St. Martin's Press, 1992.

Trento, Joseph J. *Prelude to Terror.* New York: Carroll & Graf, 2005.

Wallis, Jim. *God's Politics.* New York: Harper San Francisco, Division of Harper Collins, 2005.

Whitlock, Craig. "The Architect of the New War on the West," in *The Washington Post,* May 23, 2006. http://www.msnbc.msn.com/id/12914965.

Whitman, Christine Todd. *It's My Party, Too.* New York: Penguin Press, 2005.

Wilber, Ken. *Boomeritis.* Boston: Shambala, 2002.

Wilber, Ken. *Marriage of Sense and Soul.* New York: Broadway Book, 1998.

Wilber, Ken. *A Theory of Everything,* Boston: Shambala, 2000.

Williams, Bob and Jindrich, Morgan. "On the Road Again—and Again, Report for The Center for Public Integrity." Published at http://www.openairwaves.org/telecom/report.aspx?aid=15.

Online Resources

All sites accessed September 30, 2006.

http://www.reclaimdemocracy.org
http://www.spiritone.com
http://www.ratical.org
http://www.mcn.org/e/iii/afd/santaclara.html.
http://www.fordham.edu/halsall/mod/mussolini-fascism.html
http://www.worldfuturefund.org/wffmaster/Reading/Germany/
    mussolini.htm
http://www.historyguide.org/europe/duce.html
http://www.freepress.org
http://www.uscountvotes.org
http://www.blackboxvoting.org
http://www.erisk.com/Learning/CaseStudies/
    USSavingsLoanCrisis.asp#NOTES
http://www.wto.org/english/thewto_e/whatis_e/inbrief_e/
    inbr00_e.htm
http://www.brettonwoods.org/
http://www.reclaimdemocracy.org/personhood/#significant

FREE Discussion Guide

Many groups are using *Call to Liberty* as the basis of the discussion and study. Get your free discussion guide at http://www.calltoliberty.net. Just register with your email address, and we'll automatically send the discussion guide in PDF format.

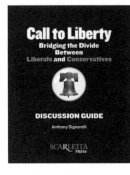

★

If you would like to invite Anthony to speak with your group, please contact us at events@calltoliberty.net.

★

Anthony blogs regularly at http://www.calltoliberty.net. Please join him there and share your ideas, thoughts, and insights about the body politic of America.